MIX
Papier aus verantwortungsvollen Quellen
Paper from responsible sources
FSC® C105338

Sharon Mutsau

Revisiting Bilateral Investment Treaties in the 21st Century

A Kenyan and South African Experience

Anchor Academic
Publishing

Mutsau, Sharon: Revisiting Bilateral Investment Treaties in the 21st Century. A Kenyan and South African Experience, Hamburg, Anchor Academic Publishing 2017

Buch-ISBN: 978-3-96067-169-5
PDF-eBook-ISBN: 978-3-96067-669-0
Druck/Herstellung: Anchor Academic Publishing, Hamburg, 2017

Bibliografische Information der Deutschen Nationalbibliothek:
Die Deutsche Nationalbibliothek verzeichnet diese Publikation in der Deutschen Nationalbibliografie; detaillierte bibliografische Daten sind im Internet über http://dnb.d-nb.de abrufbar.

Bibliographical Information of the German National Library:
The German National Library lists this publication in the German National Bibliography. Detailed bibliographic data can be found at: http://dnb.d-nb.de

Dedication

I dedicate this thesis to my mother, Enivah Mutsau who has been my greatest mentor and supporter throughout my entire life.

Acknowledgments

First and for most I would like to thank the Lord Almighty for his blessings upon my life without which I would have never been able to accomplish this goal neither would I even have had the opportunity. It is by God's grace that I have come this far.

I am heavily indebted to Prof Rieke Wandrag, my supervisor, for all her guidance and support throughout my writing. As she is the co-ordinator of the LLM programme I am also grateful for her approval of my application to join the programme.

I am also grateful for my mother's unfailing support throughout my life. Not only has she been there to support my every financial need and moral upbringing but she has also been my greatest source of inspiration. She has taught me the importance of putting God first in all that we do, the importance of education and the desire to never give up, lessons that have enabled me to reach this academic milestone.

I am also grateful to my sisters Nyasha and Fungisai Chambwe who have set good examples for me to follow. There have also been there to read through the numerous drafts of this research and provided me with the moral support I needed to pull through with the research.

I am also indebted for all those that encouraged me throughout my studies. To this end I would like to thank my father, Tafadzwa and Moreblessing Mutsau, my best friends Tafadzwa Maidza, Rutendo and Karen Manyati and all my classmates in the LLM in Trade, Investment and Business Law programme of 2014-2015 with special mention to Salome Chapeyama for her ideas and contributions in my research.

God bless you all.

Table of Contents

List of Acronyms

AILA	African International Legal Awareness
BEE	Black Economic Empowerment
BIT	Bilateral Investment Treaty
BRICS	Brazil, Russia, India, China, South Africa
B-BBEEA	Broad-Based Black Economic Empowerment Act 53 of 2003
COMESA	Common Market for Eastern and Southern Africa
CCIA	COMESA Common Investment Area
DTI	Department of Trade and Industry
EAC	East African Community
EPZ	Export Processing Zone
EPZA	Export Processing Zone Act
FDI	Foreign Direct Investment
FIPA	Foreign Investment Protection Act
FTA	Free Trade Area
GDP	Gross Domestic Product
HDSA	Historically Disadvantaged South Africans
ICSID	International Convention on the Settlement of Investment Disputes
IISD	International Institute for Sustainable Development
IIA	International Investment Agreements
IMF	International Monetary Fund
IMC	Inter Ministerial Committee
ISDS	Investor-State Dispute Settlement

MPRDA	Mineral and Petroleum Resource Development Act of 2004
MFN	Most Favoured Nation
NAFTA	North American Free Trade Agreement
NT	National Treatment
OECD	Organisation for Economic Co-operation and Development
PPIB	Promotion and Protection of Investment Bill
SADC	Southern Africa Development Community
Tralac	Trade Law Centre for Southern Africa
UK	United Kingdom
UNCTAD	United Nations Conference on Trade and Development
VAT	Value Added Tax
WBES	World Business Environment Survey

Chapter 1: Introduction

1.1 Background

A Bilateral Investment Treaty (BIT) is an agreement between two countries for the reciprocal encouragement, promotion and protection of investments in each other's territories by companies based in either country.[1] Most analysts believe that the purpose of the BITs is to attract Foreign Direct Investment (FDI) to the host country that is linked to economic growth while for the investor; the primary benefit is the protection that the BITs provide from the risks associated with investing in a foreign country.[2] Such protection will vary depending on the terms of a particular BIT but most model BITs share six common core provisions that seek the protection from expropriation or nationalisation, most favoured nation treatment, national treatment, repatriation and investment of earnings, observation of contractual obligations, and dispute resolution.[3]

The first ever BIT was signed between Germany and Pakistan in 1959 and entered into force in 1962.[4] Other states quickly followed the German-Pakistan example and many BITs were signed during the 1960s using a similar pattern.[5] The BITs were entered into mostly between developing and developed countries, but the trend changed in recent decades as more BITs are being entered into between developing countries.[6] Most BITs in existence in Africa were signed after the countries attained their independence. For example, after 1994 the South African government entered into a flurry of BITs with developed countries. These BITs were signed principally with European countries that were equally keen to support South Africa's transition

---

[1] United Nations Conference on Trade and Development (UNCTAD) 'Investment Instruments Online' available at *http://www.unctadxi.org/templates/Page1006.aspx* (accessed 20 February 2015).

[2] Ginsburg T 'International Substitutes for Domestic Institutions: Bilateral Investment Treaties and Governance' (2005) 25 *International Review of Law and Economics* 108.

[3] Masamba M 'Africa and bilateral investment treaties: to "BIT" or not?' available at *http://www.consultancyafrica.com/index.php?option=com_content&view=article&id=1697:africa-and-bilateral-investment-treaties-to-bit-or-not&catid=82:african-industry-a-business&Itemid=266*(accessed 20 February 2015).

[4] Ghouri A A 'The Evolution of bilateral investment treaties, investment treaty arbitration and international investment law' (2011) 14 (6) *Int. A.L.R* 196.

[5]Ghouri A A 'The Evolution of bilateral investment treaties, investment treaty arbitration and international investment law' (2011) 14 (6) *Int. A.L.R* 196.

[6] Masamba M 'Africa and bilateral investment treaties: to "BIT" or not?' available at *http://www.consultancyafrica.com/index.php?option=com_content&view=article&id=1697:africa-and-bilateral-investment-treaties-to-bit-or-not&catid=82:african-industry-a-business&Itemid=266*(accessed 20 February 2015).

from apartheid, back into the community of nations, with a view of encouraging foreign investment in the new South Africa.[7] Many countries followed a similar approach resulting in 1472 BITs being signed within the 1990s.[8] Many of these BITs are still in force in this 21st century.

In recent years, there has been criticism regarding the BITs that were signed prior to the 21st century that are still in force to date. As highlighted, by South Africa, for example, in the desire to attract foreign investment, insufficient heed was paid to the less obvious, and less attractive, consequences of those treaties.[9] It is also argued that BITs restrict the policy space of a host state in favour of foreign investors.[10] Host states have given up their sovereign right to pursue policy objectives due to the BITs that they signed. In addition, BITs have also been regarded as affording investors preference with corporate rights over public interest.[11] Some lawyers believe that the first wave of BITs was signed too fast with text penned by a closely-knit group of western lawyers.[12] Based on this belief, it is concluded that the majority of BITs reflect the texts developed to promote the 1960s anti-communist, post-decolonisation protection agenda for European investors.[13]

In addition to the criticism of BITs that has been highlighted, it is also important to include the fact that the number of cases brought to the International Convention for the Settlement of Investment Disputes (ICSID) has also increased in the last decade.

---

[7]Lang J 'Bilateral Investment Treaties- a shield or a sword?' available at *http://www.bowman.co.za/FileBrowser/ArticleDocuments/South-African-Government-Canceling-Bilateral-Investment-Treaties.pdf*(accessed 20 February 2015).

[8]Lang J 'Bilateral Investment Treaties- a shield or a sword?' available at *http://www.bowman.co.za/FileBrowser/ArticleDocuments/South-African-Government-Canceling-Bilateral-Investment-Treaties.pdf*(accessed 20 February 2015).

[9]Lang J 'Bilateral Investment Treaties- a shield or a sword?' available at *http://www.bowman.co.za/FileBrowser/ArticleDocuments/South-African-Government-Canceling-Bilateral-Investment-Treaties.pdf*(accessed 20 February 2015).

[10] Masamba M 'Africa and bilateral investment treaties: to "BIT" or not?' available at *http://www.consultancyafrica.com/index.php?option=com_content&view=article&id=1697:africa-and-bilateral-investment-treaties-to-bit-or-not&catid=82:african-industry-a-business&Itemid=266*(accessed 20 February 2015).

[11] Masamba M 'Africa and bilateral investment treaties: to "BIT" or not?' available at *http://www.consultancyafrica.com/index.php?option=com_content&view=article&id=1697:africa-and-bilateral-investment-treaties-to-bit-or-not&catid=82:african-industry-a-business&Itemid=266*(accessed 20 February 2015).

[12]Green AR 'Bilateral investment treaties coming back to bite' available at *http://www.thisisafricaonline.com/Business/Legal-Bulletin/Bilateral-investment-treaties-coming-back-to-bite*(accessed 20 February 2015).

[13] Green AR 'Bilateral investment treaties coming back to bite' available at *http://www.thisisafricaonline.com/Business/Legal-Bulletin/Bilateral-investment-treaties-coming-back-to-bite*(accessed 20February 2015).

In the year 2000, there were less than 10 cases reported at ICSID but by the year 2013, investors had initiated at least 57 known investor-state dispute settlement cases pursuant to International Investment Agreements (IIAs).[14] This number came close to the highest number of cases that has ever been reported in a single year at ICSID.[15] Some of the cases that were brought before the court included challenges to a broad range of government measures, including changes related to investment incentive schemes, alleged breaches of contracts, alleged direct or *de facto* expropriation, revocation of licenses or permits, regulation of energy tariffs, allegedly wrongful criminal prosecution, land zoning decisions, invalidation of patents and many more.[16] The issues raised in these cases do not only indicate that BITs create risks that may result in dispute settlement proceedings but also indicate the potential for huge financial costs being incurred when disputes arise. The dispute mechanism could also be viewed as an infringement of the host countries sovereignty as disputes are settled in international tribunals and not the domestic courts.[17]

In order to address concerns raised in some of these disputes, some countries have embarked on reviewing their BITs. These countries include the USA, Norway, Canada, South Africa and other states to mention a few.[18] Other countries such as Bolivia, Ecuador and Venezuela, have been very vocal in challenging investment protection regimes and have either terminated their BITs or have even gone as far as withdrawing from ICSID.[19] In March of 2014, Indonesia decided to terminate its BIT with the Netherlands as of 1 July 2015 and has also indicated that it intends to terminate all of its 67 BITs.[20]

---

[14] UNCTAD 'Recent developments in investor-state disputes ISDS' Issue note number 1 April 2014 available at *http://unctad.org/en/publicationslibrary/webdiaepcb2014d3_en.pdf*(accessed 20 February 2015).
[15] UNCTAD 'Recent developments in investor-state disputes ISDS' Issue Note number 1 April 2014 available at *http://unctad.org/en/publicationslibrary/webdiaepcb2014d3_en.pdf*(accessed 20 February 2015).
[16] UNCTAD 'Recent developments in investor-state disputes ISDS' Issue Note number 1 April 2014 available at *http://unctad.org/en/publicationslibrary/webdiaepcb2014d3_en.pdf*(accessed 20 February 2015).
[17] Green AR 'Bilateral investment treaties coming back to bite' available at *http://www.thisisafricaonline.com/Business/Legal-Bulletin/Bilateral-investment-treaties-coming-back-to-bite*(accessed 20 February 2015).
[18] Green AR 'Bilateral investment treaties coming back to bite' available at *http://www.thisisafricaonline.com/Business/Legal-Bulletin/Bilateral-investment-treaties-coming-back-to-bite*(accessed 20 February 2015).
[19] Cotula L 'Is the tide turning for Africa's investment treaties?' available at *http://www.iied.org/tide-turning-for-africa-s-investment-treaties*(accessed 20 February 2015).
[20] Hovells, Nesbitt, Gonzalez et al 'Indonesia terminates its Bilateral Investment Treaties (BIT) with the Netherlands from the 1st of July 2015 and may terminate all of its BIT's' available at

The majority of countries that signed the 1472 BITs that came into force in the 1990s have not taken any action toward reviewing their BITs. Kenya is an example that currently has four BITs that were signed prior to the 21st century and date back to as early as 1970. These BITs have still not been subject to review. During the release of the 2014 Trade and Development Report, the United Nations Conference on Trade and Development (UNCTAD) Secretary General Dr Mukhisa Kituyi, urged the Kenyan government to consider renegotiating decade-old bilateral agreements, arguing that they favour foreign investors at the expense of locals.[21] In his speech, Dr Kituyi indicated that South Africa had set an example by going full-blown in throwing out decade-old agreements that favoured foreign investors thereby enabling it to rethink the agreements in a way that favours local industries.[22]

1.2 Problem Statement

The fact that some countries such as Kenya have not revisited the BITs that they signed prior to the 21st century presents a problem in itself given all the criticisms about the BITs highlighted above. Host countries need to be certain that the agreements they entered into decades ago are still reflective of the very same purpose that they sought when they signed the BITs. Moreover, the BITs should not create consequences detrimental to the host country that they did not envision when they signed the BITs. Countries such as Kenya should, therefore, revisit their BITs to see whether there are any problems emanating from them that they need to address. Given the fact that South Africa, among other countries, has already reviewed its BITs, Kenya may have to learn from South Africa's experience in coming up with a solution for its problems regarding its BITs. This thesis, seeks to highlight the problems with Kenya's BITs that were signed prior to the 21st century while taking lessons from South Africa's experience and recommending a course of action for the Kenyan government.

---

http://www.lexology.com/library/detail.aspx?g=2a596886-3ad2-464b-a510-ab3b0cff503b (accessed 20 February 2015).

[21] Kariuki J 'Kenya told to review bilateral trade agreements' available at *http://www.nation.co.ke/business/Kenya-told-to-review-trade-deals/-/996/2452122/-/hwnj81/-/index.html*(accessed 20 February 2015).

[22] Kariuki J 'Kenya told to review bilateral trade agreements' available at *http://www.nation.co.ke/business/Kenya-told-to-review-trade-deals/-/996/2452122/-/hwnj81/-/index.html*(accessed 20 February 2015).

1.3 Significance of the study

BITs signed prior to the 21st century are problematic. Some countries with BITs signed during this period have since reviewed those BITs and taken action to address the disadvantages the BITs held for the host nation or have either resorted to eradicating some of their BITs. In particular, developing countries that signed BITs with developed nations seem to be disproportionately disadvantaged in these agreements. This thesis highlights Kenya's current BIT situation and compares it in light of another developing country, South Africa, with regards to its BIT experience. Given that South Africa has undergone an extensive BIT review process and moves to change some of these BITs, this thesis compares and contrasts the Kenyan and South African experience. The study highlights the possible lessons that could be learnt from the South African BIT review experience and provides recommendations for the Kenyan government regarding its outdated BITs. The lessons and recommendations benefit not only Kenya but also other countries that are still to review their BITs as it adds to the literature on why it is important for countries with such BITs to revisit them and how best they can go about the review mechanism. In addition, the study is also significant in that it raises awareness of the use and effects of BITs, thereby enabling countries that enter into such agreements to make informed decisions.

1.4 Research Question

Based on the problem that has been highlighted above, and the underlying assumption that Kenya needs to revisit its BITs, this thesis will answer the following primary question: How should Kenya revisit its BITs and what is the course of action for Kenya?

In answering this question, other sub-questions will also need to be answered which are:

i. What are the legal problems with the current BITs in Kenya that were signed prior to the 21st century and how may they affect Kenya?
ii. What prompted South Africa to review its BITs and how did they proceed in reviewing the BITs.
iii. What were the results of South Africa's review process and what measures were adopted?
iv. What lessons could Kenya learn from the South African experience and what is the recommended course of action for Kenya?

1.5 Methodology

The methodology used in developing this research is a desk and library literature study. This research is a comparative study with South Africa as the comparator due to the fact that South Africa is an example of a country that has reviewed its BITs and could provide guidance on the review mechanism for Kenya as well as providing lessons that Kenya could utilise in reviewing its BITs. The primary sources used in the research are mostly the BITs of both Kenya and South Africa together with several Acts of Parliament of both countries that have a bearing on the countries respective BITs. The secondary sources include books on international investment law, internet sources, journal articles and other publications.

1.6 Chapter Outline

This thesis comprises of five chapters.

Chapter 1

This chapter introduces the thesis with a background, the problem statement, the significance of the study, the research questions, the methodology and the chapter outline of the study.

Chapter 2

This chapter focuses on the BITs signed by Kenya prior to the 21st Century. There are four BITs that Kenya signed during this period. Each BIT will be analysed comprehensively in the context of Kenya's domestic legislative framework or domestic policies. The aim of the analysis is to examine the potential for legal problems that may arise from the BITs and how such problems might pose legal challenges for Kenya.

Chapter 3

This chapter will briefly introduce South Africa's BIT history followed by a description of the factors that prompted South Africa to review its BITs, the manner in which South Africa reviewed its BITs and the measures that South Africa implemented after review. The main focus will also be on the BITs that were signed prior to the 21stcentury by South Africa in order to provide a basis for comparison with the Kenyan situation.

Chapter 4

This chapter will compare the situation that exists in Kenya now, which has a bearing on its outdated BITs, to the situation that existed in South Africa prior to review. The aim would be to identify the factors that could also prompt Kenya to initiate a review process of its BITs. In addition, this chapter will highlight the possible lessons that Kenya could learn from South Africa's experience.

Chapter 5

This chapter will provide recommendations and the course of action for Kenya. It will also be the concluding chapter of the thesis.

1.7 Definition of keywords

Bilateral Investment Treaty: An agreement between two countries for the reciprocal encouragement, promotion and protection of investments in each other's territories by companies based in either country.[23]

Foreign Direct Investment: The transfer of tangible or intangible assets from one country to another for the purpose of their use in that country to generate wealth under the total or partial control of the owner of the assets[24]

International Investment Agreements: Treaties between states that exist in three primary forms that are bilateral investment treaties, regional investment treaties and chapters of integrated trade and investment agreements that can be signed at the bilateral or regional level.[25]

Promotion and Protection of Investment Bill: This proposed Bill is meant to provide for the legislative protection of investors and the protection and promotion of investment; to achieve a balance of rights and obligations that apply to all investors; and to matters connected therewith.[26]

---

[23] UNCTAD 'Investment Instruments Online' available at *http://www.unctadxi.org/templates/Page1006.aspx* (accessed 20 February 2015).

[24] Sornarajah M *The International Law on Foreign Investment* 3 ed (2012) 8.

[25] Mann H 'International Investment Agreements, Business and Human Rights: Key Issues and Opportunities' 2008 *IISD* 3.

[26] The *Protection and Promotion of Investment Bill* (GN 1087 in GG 36995 of 1November 2013).

Chapter 2: Potential legal problems in Kenya's BITs

2.0 Introduction

This chapter focuses on the four BITs signed by Kenya prior to the 21st Century. These BITs were signed with the Netherlands in 1970, Germany in 1996, Italy in 1996 and the United Kingdom (UK) together with Northern Ireland (hereinafter referred to as the UK BIT) in 1999.[27] Each BIT will be analysed individually with further comprehensive analyses in the context of Kenya's domestic legislative framework or domestic policies. The aim of this analysis is to examine the potential legal problems that may arise from such BITs and how such problems could pose legal challenges for Kenya.

2.1 Brief overview of Kenya's BITs signed prior to the 21st Century

Kenya's model BIT makes provisions for generally the same terms and does not deviate significantly from the typical modern BIT highlighted in the previous chapter. Allee and Peinhardt point out that there is a fallacy promoted that BITs are uniform when, in fact, each treaty has an internal balance that has been negotiated by the parties.[28] Based on this fact, the four BITs signed by Kenya have minor differences indicating the varying interests or concerns of the parties that negotiated with Kenya. The differences mainly emanate from the manner in which the same provisions are phrased in the different BITs. There is also evidence of certain provisions found in certain Kenyan BITs that are not found in the others. With this in mind, the following section shall focus on analysing the provisions of the four BITs signed prior to the 21st century in order to determine potential problems for the Kenyan government.

2.2 Analyses of Kenya's BITs based on legal interpretation

This section will focus on the provisions relating to the definition of terms, the fair and equitable treatment, the protection and security standard, the national treatment and most favoured nation clause, the investor-state dispute resolution provision and the provisions that refer to a contracting party's national legislation particularly focused

---

[27] UNCTAD 'Investment policy hub' available at *http://investmentpolicyhub.unctad.org/IIA/CountryBits/108*(accessed 3 March 2015).

[28] Allee T & Peinhardt C 'Delegating Differences: Bilateral Investment Treaties and Bargaining Over Dispute Resolution Provision' (2010) 54 *International Studies Quarterly* 2.

on the legal interpretation of the BITs. This analysis will search for potential problem areas in Kenya's BITs entered into prior to the 21st century.

2.2.1 Definition of terms

The terms defined in Kenya's BITs are not uniformly provided neither are they defined in similar terms. Despite such differences, all four BITs do, however, try to define at least either the term 'investment' or 'investor'. The definition of the terms 'investment' and 'investor' are important because, from the perspective of a capital exporting country, the definition identifies the group of investors whose foreign investment the country is seeking to protect through the agreement, including, in particular, its system for neutral and depoliticised dispute settlement.[29] From the capital importing country's perspective, it identifies the investors and the investments the country wishes to attract and from the investor's perspective, it identifies the way in which the investment might be structured in order to benefit from the agreements' protection.[30]

Only the Netherlands, Germany and Italian BITs define who the investor is.[31] These three BITs define investor with reference to the term 'nationals' or 'natural person', and 'company' or 'legal person'. The definition of the term 'national' or 'natural person' in the three treaties merely requires that nationality be determined in terms of the laws of the country that the national claims to be from. This proves problematic in that it results in situations in which foreign investors who are not privy to the original BIT may seek to exploit the shortcomings of this definition by altering their nationality so that they benefit from the rights and protection offered under Kenya's BITs. Examples of such situations have been evident in cases such as that of *Waguih Siag v The Arab Republic of Egypt*.[32] This case involved a situation in which an Egyptian national, who had investments in Egypt, lost his Egyptian nationality at a time when he had acquired Lebanese and Italian nationality in a manner that appeared to have been devised.[33] The said claimant went on to claim under the BIT

---

29 Yannaca-Small C 'Definition of Investor and Investment in International Investment Agreements' 2008 *OECD*9.
30 Yannaca-Small C 'Definition of Investor and Investment in International Investment Agreements' 2008 *OECD*9.
31 Netherlands 14 (a) & (b), Germany Article 1 (3) & (4) and Italy Article 1 (2),(3) & (4).
32 *Waguih Elie George Siag and Clorinda Vecchi v The Arab Republic of Egypt* ICSID Case No. ARB/05/15.
33 Qureshi K Q C 'Bilateral Investment Treaties (BITs): The Essentials' available at www.mcnairchambers.com/media/.../InvestmentTreatyEssentials .pdf(accessed 3 March 2015).

that existed between Italy and Egypt as an Italian investor despite the fact that he had been an Egyptian national at the time the investment was made. This indicates that the manner in which the nationality requirement is phrased in Kenya's BITs has loopholes that may allow foreign investors from other countries that do not have BITs with Kenya to nonetheless benefit from Kenya's BITs. This presents a potential problem that may affect the Kenyan government in the event that investors from countries that do not have a BIT with Kenya devise methods to alter their nationality so that they take advantage of the protection offered by the Kenyan BITs.

The UK BIT totally excludes the definition of the term 'investor'. This gives rise to the possibility of a broad range of interpretations of who may be considered as the investor. Without the definition of such a term in the treaty, it would be difficult to prevent investors from expanding the scope of International Investment Agreement's (IIAs) protection beyond that intended by the parties to the treaty.[34]

Article 1 (a) of the UK BIT, Article 1 (1) of the Germany BIT and Article 1 (1) of Italy BIT define the term investment broadly by indicating that the term refers to any kind of asset and further lists the assets that are considered as investments. Such definitions conform to Peterson's view regarding some investment treaties that he claims to have been crafted in deliberately vague language, so as to cover the broadest range of investment situations.[35] All three definitions of the term investment in Kenya's BITs further state that the highlighted list is not exclusive. Malik states that, such a non-exclusive definition was developed by capital exporting states to ensure that a wide variety of their investors' assets were protected in the territories of their capital importing treaty partners.[36] This presents problems in that the non-exclusive list could be interpreted to include anything from foreigners' money in a bank account, a holiday home, a company's goodwill, even contracts for the sale of goods manufactured by the investor in its home country, or services performed by the investor in its home country and then sold to consumers in the host country, to mention a few examples.[37] Such assets would have little to no contribution to the

[34]Bernasconi-Osterwalder N & Johnson L 'Belgium's Model Bilateral Investment Treaty: A Review' 2010 *International Institute For Sustainable Development (IISD)*9.
[35]Peterson L 'Bilateral Investment Treaties and Development Policy-Making' 2004 *IISD*27.
[36]Malik M 'Recent Developments in the Definitions of Investment in International Investment Agreements' 2008 *IISD*7.
[37] Bernasconi-Osterwalder N & Johnson L 'Commentary to the Austrian Model Investment Treaty' 2011 *IISD 7*.

host state's economy or sustainable development and yet would still benefit from the heightened rights and protections offered by the investment agreement.[38]

The Italian BIT sought to place a limitation on the interpretation of the definition of investment by highlighting that the investment must be made in conformity with the laws and regulations of a contracting party.[39] Yackee refers to such provisions as 'in accordance to' provisions and he is of the opinion that, relying on such provisions in BITs to provide tribunals with authority to take account of the issues in dispute would pose a number of interpretative and applicative uncertainties.[40] He goes on to point out that such provisions typically do not mention which laws and regulations must be complied with.[41] Kenya's Foreign Investment Protection Act (FIPA) is an example of Kenyan legislation that may be used in interpreting the BIT provisions relating to what constitutes an investment in Kenya. This Act provides that, for an investment to be approved it has to promote the economic development of the country or would need to be of benefit to Kenya.[42] The application of this Act in the event of a dispute is not automatic not only because of the fact that it is not specifically mentioned in the treaties but also because of the manner in which tribunals have interpreted the 'in accordance to' provisions in BIT arbitrations.

In the case of *Saipem S.p.A v Bangladesh*, the tribunal indicated that Article 1 (1) of the BIT in issue that stated that investment had to be made in conformity with the laws and regulations of the host state does not limit the definition of investment under the treaty to investment within the laws and regulations of Bangladesh.[43] In *Tokios Tokeles v Ukraine*, the tribunal refused the respondent states argument that the technical defects in the restriction of the investment under Ukraine law denied the investment protection of the treaty.[44] The dissenting arbitrator in the case of *Fraport v The Republic of Philippines* in dealing with the 'in accordance to' provision, indicated that since the claimant's shareholdings constituted an investment covered

[38] Bernasconi-Osterwalder N & Johnson L 'Commentary to the Austrian Model Investment Treaty' 2011 *IISD*7.
[39]Art 1 (1) Italy BIT
[40] Yackee J W 'Investment Treaties and Investor Corruption: An Emerging Defence for Host States?' (2011-2012) 52 *Va. J. Int'l L. 723*740.
[41] Yackee J W 'Investment Treaties and Investor Corruption: An Emerging Defence for Host States?' (2011-2012) 52 *Va. J. Int'l L. 723*740.
[42] Foreign Investment Protection Act 35 of 1964 Article 3 (1) & (2).
[43]Yannaca-Small C 'Definition of Investor and Investment in International Investmnet Agreements' 2008 *OECD*77.
[44]Malik M 'Recent Developments in the Definitions of Investment in International Investment Agreements' 2008 *IISD*16.

by the BIT in issue, the requirement that the investment shall be accepted in accordance with the Philippine law could not be interpreted as a jurisdictional bar.[45]

All three of these cases indicate that the tribunal at ICSID may have jurisdiction regarding issues that may not even be considered as an investment in Kenya. This may be the case regardless of the fact that the majority decision in the Fraport case dismissed the case on the grounds that the investment had not been made in accordance with the relevant national laws.[46] There is no rule of binding precedent in international investment law,[47] and as such, tribunals may reach their own conclusions regarding the facts of a case. With such uncertainties, it is a risk for Kenya to maintain the provision in its current phrasing since it may result in interpretations that may not be in its favour.

To add to the complexity of such broad definitions or a failure to define the term investment, it is important to highlight that foreign investors often make their investments through subsidiary companies incorporated under the laws of the host state.[48] Without a specific agreement to the contrary, a locally incorporated subsidiary will not be able to bring a treaty claim against the host state.[49] However, the foreign investor shareholder can bring a claim under an applicable treaty for damages with respect to its shareholdings.[50] This has been evident in a number of cases against Argentina including the case of *CMS Gas Transmission Co. v Argentina.*[51] In this case, the ICSID Annulment Committee noted that 'the definition in the Argentina-US BIT which provided for "every kind of investment...owned or controlled directly or indirectly...such as equity, debt..." was very broad, and confirmed that investments made by minority shareholders are covered by the actual language of the definition as is also recognised by ICSID arbitral tribunals in

[45]Yannaca-Small C 'Definition of Investor and Investment in International Investmnet Agreements' 2008 *OECD*77.
[46]Yannaca-Small C 'Definition of Investor and Investment in International Investmnet Agreements' 2008 *OECD*77.
[47] Butler N 'The State of International Investment Arbitration: the possibility of establishing an appeal mechanism' (unpublished Ph.D thesis, The University of Leeds,2012) 97.
[48]Malik M 'Recent Developments in the Definitions of Investment in International Investment Agreements' 2008 *IISD*17.
[49]Malik M 'Recent Developments in the Definitions of Investment in International Investment Agreements' 2008 *IISD*17.
[50]Malik M 'Recent Developments in the Definitions of Investment in International Investment Agreements' 2008 *IISD*17.
[51] Bernasconi-Osterwalder N & Johnson L 'Commentary to the Austrian Model Investment Treaty' 2011 *IISD 8.*

comparable cases.'[52] The wording in this Argentina-US BIT is almost similar to that found in Kenya's BITs. Argentina argued, in relevant part, that if the tribunals allowed minority or indirect shareholders to bring claims for relief based on damage to the company, host countries would be faced with a multitude of claims from different shareholders, as well as claims by the company itself.[53] The tribunals, however, rejected those arguments in favour of a broad definition of investments and in doing so; they hung their decisions on the observation that there was nothing in the actual text of the governing treaties that imposed such a limitation.[54] This indicates that Argentina had no intention of including minority shareholders as investments in its BITs and yet due to the phrasing of the definition of investment, the tribunal allowed such minority shareholders to bring a claim against Argentina. Kenya could also be subject to similar situations since Kenya's BITs that define the term investment, provide the same broad definition of the term as that found in the Argentine-US BIT that was at issue in the aforementioned case.

2.2.2 Fair and equitable treatment

The fair and equitable treatment is the second most important and common feature of BITs after the expropriation clause that is found in almost every BIT.[55] The Netherlands BIT provides that:

> 'each contracting party shall ensure fair and equitable treatment to the investments, goods, rights and interests of nationals of the other contracting party and shall not impair the management, maintenance, use, enjoyment or disposal thereof by those nationals, by unjustified or discriminatory measures.'[56]

This provision is also similar to that of Article 2 in the Germany, Italy and UK BITs. However, all four BITs fail to elaborate what the term fair and equitable treatment entails.

---

[52]Malik M 'Recent Developments in the Definitions of Investment in International Investment Agreements' 2008 *IISD*18.

[53] Bernasconi-Osterwalder N & Johnson L 'Commentary to the Austrian Model Investment Treaty' 2011 *IISD 8.*

[54] Bernasconi-Osterwalder N & Johnson L 'Commentary to the Austrian Model Investment Treaty' 2011 *IISD 8.*

[55]Malik M 'Time for a Change. Germanys Bilateral Investment Treaty Programme and Development Policy' (2006) 27 *Dialogue on Globalisation Occasional Paper* 22.

[56] Agreement on Economic Co-operation between the Government of the Kingdom of the Netherlands and the Government of the Republic of Kenya of 1970 Article 7.

According to Peterson, investment arbitration can be plagued by a troubling lack of consistency in the interpretation of the substantive provisions in BITs from one case to the next.[57] This is further supported by Schreuer, who states that with regards to the fair and equitable provision, the meaning will often depend on the specific circumstances of the case at hand.[58] In *S.D Myers v Canada, Metalclad v Mexico and Pope and Talbot v Canada*, three tribunals provided three radically different interpretations of the same North American Free Trade Agreement (NAFTA) fair and equitable treatment clause.[59] With such uncertainties on how the provision in Kenya's BITs may be interpreted in the event of a dispute, it is a risk for Kenya to maintain the provision as it is without a further elaboration of the term.

Furthermore, in cases involving Ukraine and Argentina regarding the fair and equitable treatment standard, the tribunals found that both governments had breached the standard by undermining the legitimate expectations of the investors.[60] The conclusions reached in these cases involving the two governments indicate that the governments were unaware of what the foreign investors' expectations were regarding the interpretation of the fair and equitable clause. As such, it is evident that without a clear explanation of what the fair and equitable treatment entails, the Kenyan government risks legal action from investors whose expectations of the provision may differ from what the Kenyan government envisaged when entering into these BITs.

2.2.3 Protection and security clause

The Germany BIT in Article 4 (1) and the UK BIT in Article 2 (2) provide that investments by nationals or companies of either contracting party shall enjoy full protection and security in the territory of the other. Green is of the view that this provision puts a hefty responsibility on the state to ensure that foreign investors'

---

[57] Peterson L 'Bilateral Investment Treaties and Development Policy-Making' 2004 *IISD*27.

[58] Schreuer C 'Fair and Equitable Treatment in Arbitral Practice' (2005) 6 *The Journal of World Investment and Trade*

[59] Butler N 'The State of International Investment Arbitration: the possibility of establishing an appeal mechanism' (unpublished Ph.D thesis, The University of Leeds,2012) 91.

[60] Haftel Y &Thompson A *When Do States Renegotiate International Agreements? The case of Bilateral Investment Treaties*(working paper, University of Maryland 2013) 10.

investments are protected.[61] There has been evidence of this huge responsibility on host states from a number of cases including the Swiss case against South Africa in which the South African government was mandated to compensate a Swiss investor who had acquired a game reserve in South Africa that was later subject to poaching, vandalism and theft.[62] Algeria was also taken to tribunals to pay damages related to civil unrest during the civil war.[63] Congo also faced claims for riots on the streets of Kinshasa.[64] This presents a problem for Kenya in that; Kenya has security concerns that emanate from its neighboring country Somalia.[65] Most notable has been the attack at Garrissa University College that occurred in April of 2015.[66] Also of note, an attack in September 2013 on the prominent West Gate shopping mall that resulted in damage to property and left 71 people dead.[67] Other security-threatening incidents occurred in 2010 and 2011 in which there were grenade attacks on a Nairobi nightclub, a bus station, refugee camps and towns near the Somalia border.[68] Reports indicate that to date, none of the attacks have been targeted at commercial projects or installations.[69] In the event that such attacks are made on foreign investor's property, Kenya may be obliged by its pre-21st century BITs to compensate foreign investors. This presents a potential problem in that the attacks emanate from a country that Kenya has no control over and so as such, guaranteeing protection of investors' property is a huge responsibility for the state.

---

[61] Green AR 'Bilateral investment treaties coming back to bite' available at http://www.thisisafricaonline.com/Business/Legal-Bulletin/Bilateral-investment-treaties-coming-back-to-bite(Accessed 19 October 2014).

[62] Lang J 'Bilateral Investment Treaties- a shield or a sword?' available at *http://www.bowman.co.za/FileBrowser/ArticleDocuments/South-African-Government-Canceling-Bilateral-Investment-Treaties.pdf* (accessed 3 March 2015).

[63] Green AR 'Bilateral investment treaties coming back to bite' available at http://www.thisisafricaonline.com/Business/Legal-Bulletin/Bilateral-investment-treaties-coming-back-to-bite(accessed 3 March 2015).

[64] Green AR 'Bilateral investment treaties coming back to bite' available at http://www.thisisafricaonline.com/Business/Legal-Bulletin/Bilateral-investment-treaties-coming-back-to-bite(accessed 3 March 2015).

[65] UNCTAD 'An Investment guide to Kenya Opportunities and Conditions ' 3.

[66] Brumfield B 'Garissa University Attack: The Problems Plaguing Kenya's Security Efforts' available at *http://edition.cnn.com/2015/04/03/africa/garissa-attacks-kenya-security/* (accessed 3 April 2015).

[67] U.S Department of State 'Investment Climate Statement 2014' available at *http://www.state.gov/e/eb/rls/othr/ics/2014/index.htm* (accessed 3 March 2015).

[68] KPMG 'Kenya country profile' available at *http://www.atilimfuar.com/en/belge/kenya.pdf* (accessed 3 March 2015).

[69] KPMG 'Kenya country profile' available at *http://www.atilimfuar.com/en/belge/kenya.pdf* (accessed 3 March 2015).

Any failure to provide protection by the Kenyan government could prove costly for the country.

2.2.4 The national treatment and most favoured nation provision

Kenya's BITs under consideration include the national treatment (NT) and the most favoured nation (MFN) clauses. The NT provision in Kenya's BITs requires the contracting parties to provide no less favourable treatment to foreign investors than it accords to its nationals. This provision applies regardless of the fact that the same foreign investors may be privy to forms of favourable treatment such as subsidies, tax holidays or regulatory exemptions that may not be afforded to local investors.[70] Not only does this create an unfair advantage to the foreign investors in this regard but it also constrains the promotion of local industries in developing countries such as Kenya which may need assistance to grow in order to compete with foreign companies.[71] Moreover, the NT provision in Kenya's BITs does not contain the 'like circumstances' clause which arguably implies that foreign investments that are not in like circumstances with the local investments in issue, could also be compared to find out whether NT has been violated.[72] This presents a potential problem for Kenya in that the provision limits the policy space of Kenya in relation to its local investments and the provision may also be broadly interpreted to include unlike investments in the event of a dispute.

The MFN clause in an investment treaty is fundamentally a promise between the two state parties to the treaty that neither state will give to investors from any third state more favorable treatment than that given to investors from the other state party to the treaty.[73] This provision has been described as a core provision of international investment agreements that provides a basic minimum for the establishment of

[70] Canada's Coalition to end Global Poverty 'Bilateral Investment Treaties: A Canadian Primer' available at http://www.ccic.ca/_files/en/what_we_do/trade_2010-04_investmt_treaties_primer_e.pdf (accessed 3 March 2015).

[71] Khisa I 'Talks on EAC-US trade, investment deal face hurdles' available at http://www.theeastafrican.co.ke/business/-investment-deal-face-hurdles/-/2560/2451498/-/item/0/-/qfferbz/-/index.html (accessed 3 March 2015).

[72] Ranjan P 'India and Bilateral Investment Treaties- A Changing Landscape' (2014) 29 *ICSID Review* 433.

[73] Cole T 'The Boundaries of Most Favored Nation Treatment in International Investment Law' (2012) 33 *Michigan Journal of International Law* 539.

equality of competitive opportunities for investors from different countries.[74] The wording of the provision in Kenya's BITs is similar in Article 3 of the Germany and Italy BITs and indicates that treatment that is awarded to nationals of third countries should also be awarded to investors from the respective BIT signatories. The provision in both these treaties further indicates that the MFN principle does not refer to

> 'the advantages and privileges which one contracting party may grant to investors of third states by virtue of membership of a customs or economic union, of a common market, of a Free Trade Area (FTA), of a multilateral economic agreement or under agreement signed in order to prevent double taxation or to facilitate cross-border trade.'[75]

Article 5 of the Netherlands BIT merely states that investors of the signatory states should not be treated less favorably than citizens of third states. The UK BIT in Article 3 does not provide a list of exceptions as do the Italy and Germany BITs do, but it indicates that, the MFN provision applies to Article 1-11 of the Agreement.

The case of *Maffezini v Spain* concerned a dispute arising from the treatment of an Argentinean investor by Spanish entities in relation to the investor's production and distribution of chemicals.[76] The claimant sought to avoid submitting the dispute to the Spanish courts for 18 months as mandated by the Argentina-Spain BIT before resorting to international arbitration.[77] The claimant argued that the Argentina-Spain BITs MFN clause should allow him to import a dispute settlement provision from the Chile-Spain BIT, which merely required that the investors observe a six-month negotiating period before filing for arbitration.[78] Spain argued that the MFN clause was confined to the investor's substantive economic treatment and did not extend to

---

[74]Ukpe A 'Applicability of the Most-Favoured-Nation Clause to Dispute Settlement Provisions in Bilateral Investment Treaties: A Uniform Approach?' (2011-2012) 11 *Centre For Energy, Petroleum and Mineral Law Policy Annual Review(CEPMLP Annual Review)* 5.

[75]Article 3 (3) Italy BIT and Article 3 (3) & (4) Germany BIT.

[76] Salomon C, Friedrich S & Latham & Watkins International Arbitration Group 'How Most Favoured Nation Clauses in Bilateral Investment Treaties Affect Arbitration' available at *http://www.lw.com/thoughtLeadership/favoured-nation-clauses-arbitration* (accessed 25 March 2015).

[77] Salomon C, Friedrich S & Latham & Watkins International Arbitration Group 'How Most Favoured Nation Clauses in Bilateral Investment Treaties Affect Arbitration' available at *http://www.lw.com/thoughtLeadership/favoured-nation-clauses-arbitration* (accessed 25 March 2015).

[78] Salomon C, Friedrich S & Latham & Watkins International Arbitration Group 'How Most Favoured Nation Clauses in Bilateral Investment Treaties Affect Arbitration' available at *http://www.lw.com/thoughtLeadership/favoured-nation-clauses-arbitration* (accessed 25 March 2015).

procedural matters.[79] The tribunal in this case held that dispute settlement procedures were inextricably related to the protection of foreign investors envisaged under the BIT and therefore, the MFN clause should be applied to give the Argentina claimant the benefit of the Chile-Spain BITs easier access to international arbitration.[80]

The case above indicates how the MFN provision has been interpreted in arbitral proceedings. The argument raised by Spain in the case indicates that Spain had not envisaged the application of the MFN provision to dispute settlement provisions and yet the tribunal came to such a conclusion. Other ICSID tribunals after the Maffezeni case dealing with the relationship between MFN clauses and dispute settlement mechanisms seem to have followed the same rationale.[81] The UK BIT clearly indicates that the provision applies to all aspects including the dispute settlement provisions. Despite the Germany and Italy BITs listing a few exceptions to the application of the provision, all three of the remaining BITs are silent on the question of applicability to dispute settlement mechanisms. This is an indication that Kenya's BITs with the exclusion of the UK BIT are not clear on whether the MFN provision applies to dispute settlement provisions or not.

With regard to the dispute settlement provisions in Kenya's BITs, the UK BIT provides a three-month waiting period for investor-state disputes while the other three BITs provide for a six-month waiting period. In the event that investors from other countries that have longer waiting periods decide to benefit from other Kenyan BITs, the MFN provisions in these BITs might be extended to the dispute settlement provisions that may not have been Kenya's intention when signing the treaty.

However, it is also important to note that the Maffezini decision and others that followed a similar approach did not go unopposed. Citing one example of *Tecmed v Mexico*, the tribunal declared that it should be presumed that the parties to a treaty specifically negotiated for the dispute settlement provisions and thus the parties

[79] Salomon C, Friedrich S & Latham & Watkins International Arbitration Group 'How Most Favoured Nation Clauses in Bilateral Investment Treaties Affect Arbitration' available at *http://www.lw.com/thoughtLeadership/favoured-nation-clauses-arbitration* (accessed 25 March 2015).

[80] Salomon C, Friedrich S & Latham & Watkins International Arbitration Group 'How Most Favoured Nation Clauses in Bilateral Investment Treaties Affect Arbitration' available at *http://www.lw.com/thoughtLeadership/favoured-nation-clauses-arbitration* (accessed 3 March 2015).

[81] Figanmese I A 'The Impact of the Maffezini Decision on the Interpretation of MFN Clauses in Investment Treaties' (2011) 8 *Ankara Law Review* 234.

would not have entered into the agreement had it not been for those provisions.[82] Ukpe indicates that ICSID jurisprudence on the applicability of the MFN provision on dispute settlement provisions has been anything but uniform in both its results and analytical methodology.[83] Normally tribunals tilt towards interpreting the intention of the parties in accordance with the general rule in Article 31 of the Vienna Convention on the Laws of Treaties.[84] Article 31 (1) of the Convention provides that a treaty shall be interpreted in good faith and in accordance with the ordinary meaning to be given to the terms of the treaty in their context and in light of its object and purpose.[85] In interpreting this provision, ICSID tribunals have returned conflicting judgments.[86] Parker concludes that more than ten years after the Maffezini decision, it is safe to say there is no longer a threat of uncertainty regarding the interpretation of the MFN provision but that in fact, the uncertainty already exists.[87] This further indicates that any tribunal may interpret the MFN provision broadly if the phrasing of the parties to the treaty does not clearly indicate how the provision is to be interpreted.

2.2.5 Investor state dispute provision

Another issue potentially faced by Kenya regarding its BITs relates to the investor-state dispute clause. This provision is found in all four of Kenya's BITs that were signed prior to the 21st century. The provision allows investors to leapfrog domestic courts and sue governments in international arbitration tribunals if there has been an alleged breach of treaty protections.[88] In other words, the provision relocates decision-making power outside the country and into international panels whose determinations can have major implications on domestic policies.[89] This has already been evident in a number of cases including the challenge against Australia from

---

[82] Parker S L 'A BIT at a Time: The Proper Extension of the MFN Clause to Dispute Settlement Provisions in Bilateral Investment Treaties' (2012) 2 *Arbitration Brief* 37.

[83] Ukpe A 'Applicability of the Most-Favoured-Nation Clause to Dispute Settlement Provisions in Bilateral Investment Treaties: A Uniform Approach?' (2011-2012) 11 *CEPMLP Annual Review* 17.

[84] Ukpe A 'Applicability of the Most-Favoured-Nation Clause to Dispute Settlement Provisions in Bilateral Investment Treaties: A Uniform Approach?' (2011-2012) 11 *CEPMLP Annual Review* 8.

[85] Vienna convention on the Laws of Treaties, 1969 (1969) 8 ILM 340.

[86] Ukpe A 'Applicability of the Most-Favoured-Nation Clause to Dispute Settlement Provisions in Bilateral Investment Treaties: A Uniform Approach?' (2011-2012) 11 *CEPMLP Annual Review* 8.

[87] Parker S L 'A BIT at a Time: The Proper Extension of the MFN Clause to Dispute Settlement Provisions in Bilateral Investment Treaties' (2012) 2 *Arbitration Brief* 57.

[88] Canada's Coalition to end Global Poverty 'Bilateral Investment Treaties: A Canadian Primer' available at*http://www.ccic.ca/_files/en/what_we_do/trade_2010-04_investmt_treaties_primer_e.pdf* (accessed 5 March 2015).

[89] Draper P 'Africa: South Africa's Termination of Bilateral Investment Treaties Featured' available at *http://allafrica.com/stories/201309301804.html* (accessed on 5 March 2015).

Philip Morris International, the tobacco group, in relation to plain packaging rules for cigarettes.[90] Germany is also being challenged by Vattenfall, the Swedish energy company, over the decision to phase out nuclear power following the Fukushima nuclear disaster in Japan.[91] Not only will this prove costly for the governments involved but it will also have a bearing on the legitimate policy initiatives of these countries. Kenya may find itself in a similar position since all of its BITs make provision for the same clause.

The risk of the investor-state dispute provision in Kenya's BITs is further compounded by the fact that it is at the request of the foreign investor that the parties go to arbitration in three of the four BITs signed by Kenya prior to the 21st century with the exclusion of the UK BIT. Article 8 (3) of the UK BIT provides that the decision to choose between arbitration or conciliation lies with the foreign investor. This provision is also found in Article 9 (3) of the Italy BIT. Not only does this affect the sovereignty of a state but it also undermines the judiciary system of the country. The Australian government in its 2004 FTA with the United States refused to countenance investor-state dispute settlement in its BIT and further made a policy excluding investor-state rules from trade agreements permanent.[92] The rationale for deciding against the inclusion of the provision was based on the reasoning that Australian courts are more than capable of enforcing domestic laws.[93] This however, was later changed by the newly elected Australian government that has included the provision in the Australia-Korea BIT.[94] Regardless of the new Australian government's position on the investor-state dispute clause, the arbitration proceedings regarding dispute resolution mechanism has been argued to be biased

---

[90] Bland B & Donnan S 'Indonesia to terminate more than 60 bilateral investment treaties' available at *http://www.ft.com/intl/cms/s/0/3755c1b2-b4e2-11e3-af92-00144feabdc0.html#axzz3WrEMIGn5* (accessed 5 March 2015).

[91] Bland B & Donnan S 'Indonesia to terminate more than 60 bilateral investment treaties' available at *http://www.ft.com/intl/cms/s/0/3755c1b2-b4e2-11e3-af92-00144feabdc0.html#axzz3WrEMIGn5* (accessed 5 March 2015).

[92] Lester S 'Improving Investment Treaties through General Exceptions Provisions: The Australian Example' available at *http://www.iisd.org/sites/default/files/publications/iisd_itn_may_2014_en.pdf* (accessed 5 March 2015).

[93] Draper P 'Africa: South Africa's Termination of Bilateral Investment Treaties Featured' available at *http://allafrica.com/stories/201309301804.html* (accessed on 5 March 2015).

[94] Lester S 'Improving Investment Treaties through General Exceptions Provisions: The Australian Example' available at *http://www.iisd.org/sites/default/files/publications/iisd_itn_may_2014_en.pdf* (accessed 5 March 2015).

towards foreign investors or powerful states.[95] Article 11 (3) of the Germany BIT stresses that the award given under such arbitrations shall be binding and shall not be subject to any appeal or remedy other than those provided for in the said convention. This highlights a great risk for the Kenyan government in the event that an investor sues the government at international arbitrations where there will be no room for appeal against decisions that the government may feel have been unjustly awarded.

2.2.6 Reference to national laws

Kenya's BITs contain provisions that specifically make reference to the applicability of national laws in matters regarding the contracting parties' rights and obligations. This is in addition to the scope that is afforded to foreign investment treaties that applies to essentially all economic activities of foreign investors by broad definitions of the term investment found in practically all of the treaties as indicated above.[96] This means that BIT provisions potentially affect nearly every aspect of the host states legal system.[97] Provisions in Kenya's BITs that refer to national legislation include Article 2 (4), Article 3 (2) and Article 12 of the Italian BIT, Article 3 of the Netherlands BIT, Article 8 of the Germany BIT and Article 11 of the UK BIT. As is indicated in these provisions, where there is evidence that the domestic legislation favours investors more than the treaty does, the domestic legislation will apply. This may present a potential legal problem for Kenya in the event that Kenya decides to reform their laws that seem to favour foreign investors.

With this in mind, it is important to note that most investors base their decision to invest in a particular country on a number of factors that include the legal and regulatory framework of the country they seek to invest in.[98] A reform of a country's legislation that favoured foreign investors at the time that the investment was made to a situation where the legislation no longer favours foreign investors may affect the

---

[95] Canada's Coalition to end Global Poverty 'Bilateral Investment Treaties: A Canadian Primer' available at*http://www.ccic.ca/_files/en/what_we_do/trade_2010-04_investmt_treaties_primer_e.pdf* (accessed 5 March 2015).

[96] Dolzer R 'The Impact of International Investment Treaties on Domestic Administrative Law' (2006) 37 *International Law and Politics*956.

[97] Dolzer R 'The Impact of International Investment Treaties on Domestic Administrative Law' (2006) 37 *International Law and Politics* 956.

[98] Williams R 'Nothing Sacred: Developing Countries and the future of International Investment Treaties' available at *http://www.iisd.org/pdf/2011/developing_countries_and_the_future_of_IIAs.pdf* (accessed 5 March 2015).

business of the foreign investor if their decision to invest in the country was based on such laws. In the Czech Republic, investors are challenging the 2011 amendments that placed a levy on electricity generated from solar power plants.[99] The investors are arguing that these amendments undercut the viability of their investments and modified the incentive regime that had been originally put in place to stimulate the use of renewable energy in the country.[100] Dolzer indicates that in such situations, the investor is entitled, in principle, to rely on the legal rights granted to him by the law as it stands at the time of the investment.[101] This highlights the potential of a legal problem for Kenya since it indicates that it may be difficult to change any laws that favour investors without provoking a legal dispute with investors who may feel as though their rights to certain entitlements are being violated. Investors generally feel threatened when governments promote policy changes that could potentially have an adverse effect on their rights and legitimate expectations.[102]

The above analysis of Kenya's BITs indicates that there are potential problems in the interpretation of the treaties and that key provisions were omitted from these agreements. Another important aspect that has been highlighted by the analysis thus far is that the BITs have a bearing on Kenya's domestic legislative framework or its policies in some way. There have been concerns that the effect of foreign investment treaties on the domestic legal system may be so severe as to be unacceptable.[103] This calls for the need for an analysis of the Kenyan BITs in the context of Kenya's legislative framework or policies.

---

[99] UNCTAD 'Recent developments in investor state disputes ISDS' Issue note number 1 April 2014 available at *http://unctad.org/en/publicationslibrary/webdiaepcb2014d3_en.pdf*(accessed 5 March 2015).

[100] UNCTAD 'Recent developments in investor state disputes ISDS' Issue note number 1 April 2014 available at *http://unctad.org/en/publicationslibrary/webdiaepcb2014d3_en.pdf*(accessed 5 March 2015).

[101] Dolzer R 'The Impact of International Investment Treaties on Domestic Administrative Law' (2006) 37 *International Law and Politics* 968.

[102] Feris J 'Challenging the Status quo- South Africa`s termination of its Bilateral Trade Agreements' available at *https://www.dlapiper.com/en/latinamerica/insights/publications/2014/12/international-arbitration-newsletter-q4-2014/challenging-the-status-quo/* (accessed 5 March 2015).

[103] Dolzer R 'The Impact of International Investment Treaties on Domestic Administrative Law' (2006) 37 *International Law and Politics* 956.

2.3 Analysis of Kenya's BITs in the context of the domestic legislative framework or policies

Kenya's BITs make specific reference to the applicability of the parties' national laws to the investments made by the respective countries. Kenya has laws and regulations that govern FDI or have an impact on foreign investors' decision to invest in Kenya. Such laws will have a direct impact on investments made in the country regardless of the fact that a BIT exists with the investor's country or not. Examples of such laws include, the Constitution of Kenya (2010), the Companies Act Chapter 486 (revised 2012), the Private Public Partnership Act No. 15 of 2013 and the Foreign Investment Protection Act Chapter 518 (revised 2012) to mention a few. A further analysis of Kenya's BITs in the context of Kenya's constitution, Kenya's mining legislative framework and policies together with that of Kenya's tax regime shall be carried out in order to determine whether there exists a potential for conflicts with Kenya's BITs.

2.3.1 Kenya's mining legislation or policies

In September of 2013, the Kenyan mining secretary announced that Kenya had revoked 42 mining licenses that had been granted between 14 January and 15 May 2013.[104] The Secretary indicated that the rationale for such a measure was based on the fact that the licenses had been improperly awarded by the previous administration during the transitional period between governments earlier that year.[105] In addition to this, it was also announced that royalties on minerals were to be increased, and the exploration drilling charges were also to be increased by more than tenfold.[106] The provisions regarding the application of licenses and the financial provisions were included in a new Bill that is set to replace the Mining Act of 1940 (Chapter 306 of the Laws of Kenya).[107]

---

[104] Holman Fenwick Willan 'Kenya- Mining Update' available at *http://www.hfw.com/downloads/HFW-Kenya-Mining-September-2013.pdf* (accessed 5 March 2015).

[105] Holman Fenwick Willan 'Kenya- Mining Update' available at *http://www.hfw.com/downloads/HFW-Kenya-Mining-September-2013.pdf* (accessed 5 March 2015).

[106] Holman Fenwick Willan 'Kenya- Mining Update' available at *http://www.hfw.com/downloads/HFW-Kenya-Mining-September-2013.pdf* (accessed on 5 March 2015).

[107] The 'Mining Bill' published in Kenya Gazette Supplement No 28 National Assembly Bills No 8.

The above-mentioned revocation of licenses and the drastic increases in royalties and drilling charges may have impacted foreign investors by creating an adverse business environment. Article 5 (1) of the Italian BIT states that

> 'the investment to which this agreement relates shall not be subject to any measure which might limit the right of ownership, possession, control or enjoyment of the investments, permanently or temporarily, save where specifically provided by current, national or local, legislation or regulations and orders handed down by courts or tribunals having jurisdiction.'

The new Mining Bill highlighted above is still set to become an Act and so it does not warrant an exception under Article 5 (1) highlighted above since the exception embodied in the BIT provision refers to current legislation existing in Kenya and not future legislation. The Bill if passed into an Act will be a violation of the said provision since it limits the rights of ownership, possession, control or enjoyment of foreign investor's investment in Kenya's mining industry. This would thereby oblige the Kenyan government to compensate Italian foreign investors.

In an article by King and Spalding, the authors indicate the same view by highlighting that, foreign mining companies that had investments in Kenya, whose mining licenses were cancelled, whose revenues decreased as a result of these new drilling charges and/or were affected by the royalty schemes may be able to bring compensation claims against the Kenyan government.[108] All these potential problems are a result of Kenya's move towards implementing reforms in the legal framework of their mining sector. Indonesia is facing a billion-dollar lawsuit from UK-listed Churchill Mining under the terms of one such treaty, in addition to several unrelated threats of costly litigation from international companies unhappy with a new mining law.[109]This highlights a need for Kenya to review its BITs that they signed prior to the 21st century in the context of its domestic legislative framework since they are moving towards making reforms in their legislation that may result in violations of their BIT obligations.

---

[108]King and Spalding Client Alert 'Recent Developments: Kenya- What legal options are available to mining companies' available at *http://www.kslaw.com/imageserver/KSPublic/library/publication/ca082013.pdf*(accessed 5 March 2015).

[109] Indonesia for Global Justice 'After South Africa, Indonesia takes a brave decision to terminate its BIT with the Netherlands' available at *http://www.bilaterals.org/?press-release-indonesia-takes-a* (accessed 5 March 2015).

2.3.2 Kenya's tax policies and measures affecting Kenya's constitution

Another area in which Kenya's legislative framework or domestic policy may affect its current BITs may be found in Kenya's tax laws in relation to foreign investments. The government of Kenya provides a wide range of tax incentives to businesses to attract greater levels of FDI into the country.[110] The Kenya Revenue Authority (KRA) defines tax incentives as a provision that grants any person or activity favourable conditions that deviate from the normal provisions of the tax legislation.[111] Often, these investment incentives are provided to companies operating in Export Processing Zones (EPZs).[112] EPZs are a secured territory where a special tax regime and other conditions are applied to companies operating therein.[113] The majority of the EPZ investors (61 percent) are foreign companies primarily from China, Britain, the US, the Netherlands, Qatar, Taiwan and India, some of which have BITs with Kenya.[114]

The EPZs are governed by the Export Processing Zone Act (EPZA) Chapter 157 of 1990. This Act makes provision for benefits to EPZ Enterprises, which among other provisions include several tax exemptions.[115] Some of the fiscal incentives that are offered to investors include a ten year corporate tax holiday and 25 percent tax rate on profits thereafter (except for commercial activities), ten year withholding tax holiday, duty and value added tax (VAT) exemption on inputs and stamp duty exemption.[116] Some analysts are of the opinion that these tax incentives are leading to very large revenue losses and are not needed to attract FDI.[117] Dr Kituyi, the

---

[110] Tax Justice Network- Africa and ActionAid International 'Tax Competition in East Africa: A Race to the Bottom? Tax incentives and revenue losses in Kenya' available at *http://www.taxjustice.net/cms/upload/pdf/kenya_report_full.pdf* (accessed 5 March 2015).

[111] Budget Information Programme Team 'The Budget Focus Issue No 30' available at *www.ieakenya.or.ke/publications/doc_download/246-tax-incentives-and-exemption-regime-in-kenya-is-it-working* (accessed 5 March 2015).

[112] Cheng, Everaert, Jonas et al *Kenya, Uganda and United Republic of Tanzania: Selected Issues* (2008) 10.

[113] Cheng, Everaert, Jonas et al *Kenya, Uganda and United Republic of Tanzania: Selected Issues* (2008) 10.

[114] Tax Justice Network- Africa and ActionAid International 'Tax Competition in East Africa: A Race to the Bottom? Tax incentives and revenue losses in Kenya' available at *http://www.taxjustice.net/cms/upload/pdf/kenya_report_full.pdf* (accessed 5 March 2015).

[115] Section 29 (1) of Export Processing Zone Act Chapter 157 of 1990.

[116] Budget Information Programme Team 'The Budget Focus Issue No 30' available at *www.ieakenya.or.ke/publications/doc_download/246-tax-incentives-and-exemption-regime-in-kenya-is-it-working* (accessed 5 March 2015).

[117] Tax Justice Network- Africa and ActionAid International 'Tax Competition in East Africa: A Race to the Bottom? Tax incentives and revenue losses in Kenya' available at *http://www.taxjustice.net/cms/upload/pdf/kenya_report_full.pdf* (accessed 5 March 2015).

UNCTAD Secretary General and Former Trade Minister of Kenya, delivered a report expressing the same view by stating that the idea that foreign companies should not be taxed in countries where they are making profits is misleading.[118] He further elaborated that there was need to strengthen the voice of the ordinary taxpayer who suffers from such tax exemptions on foreign investors.[119] These remarks were in line with Section 201 (b) (1) of the Constitution of Kenya, which encourages the burden of taxation to be shared equally.

In January 2011, the government of Kenya committed itself in its 'letter of intent' to the International Monetary Fund (IMF) to 'rationalising existing tax incentives, expanding the income base and removing tax exemptions as envisaged in the constitution'.[120] This further emphasises how the constitutional provision on the burden of taxation is being violated by the continued existence of tax incentives available to foreign investors. This may have an effect on the Kenyan government in the event that local investors or ordinary taxpayers challenge the tax regime based on the constitution.

In *Antoine Goetz and Others v The Republic of Burundi*, a Belgian investor filed a case at ICSID based on a BIT against Burundi arguing that the withdrawal of a free zone certificate granting a series of tax and customs exemptions to their investment in a precious metals business amounted to expropriation.[121] In another case *Spentex Netherlands B. V v the Republic of Uzbekistan*, the investor is complaining about the revocation of an investment incentive (a VAT subsidy).[122] Both of these cases highlight a potential problem that Kenya may experience in the event that it decides to alter its tax legislation. Investors are protected against changes in the host states policy that arbitrators may characterise as regulatory expropriation on the basis that

[118] National TV Kenya 'UNCTAD's Sec. Gen. Dr Mukhisa Kituyi calls for Kenya to review her Bilateral agreements' available at *http://mtaani.com/videochannel/43366/unctads-sec-gen-dr-mukhisa-kituyi-calls-for-kenya-to-review-her-bilateral-a/* (accessed 5 March 2015).

[119] National TV Kenya 'UNCTAD`s Sec. Gen. Dr Mukhisa Kituyi calls for Kenya to review her Bilateral agreements' available at*http://mtaani.com/videochannel/43366/unctads-sec-gen-dr-mukhisa-kituyi-calls-for-kenya-to-review-her-bilateral-a/* (accessed 5 March 2015).

[120] Tax Justice Network- Africa and ActionAid International 'Tax Competition in East Africa: A Race to the Bottom? Tax incentives and revenue losses in Kenya' available at *http://www.taxjustice.net/cms/upload/pdf/kenya_report_full.pdf* (accessed 5 March 2015).

[121] Mosoti V 'Bilateral Investment Treaties and the possibility of a multilateral framework on investment at the WTO: are poor economies caught in between' (2005) 26 *Nw. J. Int'l L. & Bus.* 123.

[122] UNCTAD 'Recent developments in investor state disputes ISDS' Issue note number 1 April 2014 available at *http://unctad.org/en/publicationslibrary/webdiaepcb2014d3_en.pdf* (accessed 5 March 2015).

a law or another measure has reduced the value of an investment.[123] As such, Kenya may not easily alter its tax regime without risking arbitration from foreign investors. Kenya is therefore restricted from implementing changes in its laws based on its BIT commitments.

All four of Kenya's BITs that are being analysed in this chapter, clearly state in the preamble that the treaties are meant for the encouragement or promotion and protection of investments. Tax incentives may be viewed as a means of promoting or encouraging investments. However, with the losses that Kenya is said to be suffering from these incentives as was highlighted above, there is need for Kenya to take measures to curb such losses and to align its tax incentives provided to foreigners with its constitution. This would involve reforms in Kenya's tax legislation that may have adverse effects on investors' business by say affecting profits or the returns from the investments that may provoke legal action against the Kenyan government. As was indicated above, countries that made the decision to invest in Kenya because of these tax incentives may be severely affected by a change in tax laws, which may lead those investors to sue the Kenyan government. It is also important to note that, issues relating to investment incentives schemes were also listed among the major disputes that were brought to ICSID.[124]

To add to the issue of tax incentives, there are many disadvantages that have been associated with them. For example, tax incentives are said to be prone to abuse when the incentive is exhausted, and the promoters of the business fraudulently wind it down and simultaneously establish another entity to be accorded the same tax incentives.[125] Such existing enterprises will disguise themselves as new enterprises through nominal reorganisation resulting in high revenue costs on the economy.[126] Some EPZ companies have also been criticised for allegedly setting up operations to benefit from the 10-year tax holiday, only to close shop at the expiry of

---

[123]Carrim X 'Lessons from South Africa`s Bilateral Investment Treaties Review' available at *http://ccsi.columbia.edu/files/2013/10/No_109_-_Carim_-_FINAL.pdf* (accessed 5 March, 2015).

[124]UNCTAD 'Recent developments in investor state disputes ISDS' Issue note number 1 May 2013 available at *http://unctad.org/en/publicationslibrary/webdiaepcb2013d3_en.pdf*(accessed 5 Macrh 2015).

[125]Tax Justice Network- Africa and ActionAid International 'Tax Competition in East Africa: A Race to the Bottom? Tax incentives and revenue losses in Kenya' available at *http://www.taxjustice.net/cms/upload/pdf/kenya_report_full.pdf* (accessed 5 March 2015).

[126] Tanzi V & Zee H 'Tax Policy for Developing Countries' available at *http://www.imf.org/external/pubs/ft/issues/issues27/* (accessed 5 March 2015).

the grace period.[127] More stringent regulatory measures need to be put in place in order to avoid such situations. In the event that such measures affect the foreign investments in the country, there would be potential legal problems for the Kenyan government.

2.4 Conclusion

This chapter examined potential legal problems that may arise from Kenya's BITs and how such problems might pose legal challenges for the country. The analysis was conducted based on the legal interpretation of the BITs and an interpretation in the context of Kenya's domestic legislative framework. What the analysis revealed was that some of Kenya's BITs omitted to define important terms and in the BITs where the terms were defined, the definitions could be subject to very broad interpretations thereby exposing the Kenyan government to unforeseen litigation. The analysis also revealed that there is not enough detail on what the fair and equitable treatment provision entails or enough detail to limit the scope of application of the most favoured nation provision that may result in undesirable interpretations for the Kenyan government. Various cases were examined, to show how the BIT provisions that were highlighted could affect Kenya, and these cases pointed out the uncertainties that plague the dispute settlement forums that are mainly used in investment disputes. Kenya's BITs were also shown to be placing a limit on the Kenyan government's policy space in matters regarding providing assistance to its own nationals due to the national treatment provision and on promulgating new legislation that affects investors' investments.

The following chapter will describe South Africa's experience with BITs entered into prior to the 21st century. It will describe the factors that prompted South Africa to review its BITs, the manner in which South Africa reviewed its BITs and the measures that South Africa took after review with particular focus on how South Africa handled some of the concerns highlighted in this chapter.

[127] Tax Justice Network- Africa and ActionAid International 'Tax Competition in East Africa: A Race to the Bottom? Tax incentives and revenue losses in Kenya' available at *http://www.taxjustice.net/cms/upload/pdf/kenya_report_full.pdf* (accessed 5 March 2015).

Chapter 3: South Africa's experience with BITs

3.0 Introduction

The chapter will focus on the BITs that were signed prior to the 21st century by South Africa. South Africa signed a total of 23 BITs during this period that came into force.[128] Of these 23 BITs, one of them was signed by South Africa's former colonial government with Paraguay in 1974 and will not be considered in this chapter. Of the 22 BITs that came into force that were signed by the post-Apartheid South African government, six of them have been terminated.[129] This chapter will indicate the factors that prompted South Africa to review its BITs, the manner in which South Africa reviewed its BITs and the measures that South Africa took after review. The focus of this chapter will not only be limited to the BITs that were terminated but on the review mechanism in general, the factors that prompted the review and the measures that South Africa took in light of that process. In so doing, this chapter will indicate the legal problems that South Africa unravelled from its BITs through the review process and the measures that it adopted after review.

3.1 Brief History of South Africa's BIT system

The first BIT that South Africa signed was with the UK in 1994. Although this BIT was signed by the new South African government in 1994, it was presented to the outgoing government in 1992/93.[130] The outgoing South African government officials simply accepted the draft model BIT without any negotiations when it was presented to them in 1992/93.[131] The rationale for such a decision can be attributed to a lot of factors including the fact that the South African government officials believed that the BIT did not conflict with any South African law and neither did it contain any

---

[128] UNCTAD 'South Africa Bilateral Investment Treaties' available at *http://investmentpolicyhub.unctad.org/IIA/CountryBits/195#iiaInnerMenu* (accessed 20 March 2015).

[129] Ruff D, Kron J & Golsong C 'Bilateral Investment Treaties in South Africa' available at *http://www.nortonrosefulbright.com/knowledge/publications/118456/bilateral-investment-treaties-in-south-africa* (accessed 20 March 2015).

[130] Williams R 'Nothing Sacred: Developing Countries and the future of International Investment Treaties' available at *http://www.iisd.org/pdf/2011/developing_countries_and_the_future_of_IIAs.pdf* (accessed 20 March 2015).

[131] Williams R 'Nothing Sacred: Developing Countries and the future of International Investment Treaties' available at *http://www.iisd.org/pdf/2011/developing_countries_and_the_future_of_IIAs.pdf* (accessed 20 March 2015).

obligations for the South African government.[132] It is important to note that this agreement and others alike entered into prior to the 21st century were negotiated without the presence of a lawyer or hardly any relevant government stakeholder.[133] Based on the beliefs that the South African government officials had at that time, the UK model BIT was adopted by South Africa as the basis for concluding 46 additional BITs (a figure inclusive of the BITs that did not come into force).[134] Most of these BITs were signed with a group of European countries that had traditionally been the largest source of FDI in South Africa.[135] The UK draft model BIT was based on a standard Organisation for Economic Co-operation and Development (OECD) model.[136] The main features of this model were that, 'it stipulated that foreign investors and their investments had to be treated fairly and equitably, there should be no discrimination or expropriation, contracts should be upheld, there should be no capital restrictions, and disputes could be adjudicated through international investor-state arbitration.'[137]

It is the opinion of Bernasconi-Osterwalder and Johnson that the OECD model provided vague, potentially strong protections for foreign investors, with little explicit consideration of the potential impacts on host states' rights, investors' obligations, or the broader relationship between investment and sustainable development.[138] At the time that this BIT was signed, South Africa was emerging from colonial rule and was yet to fully develop its strategy for negotiating BITs. In general terms, the OECD model took advantage of this situation by ensuring that capital exporters' investments benefited the most from the agreements at the expense of the capital

---

[132] Poulsen L N S 'Bounded Rationality and the Diffusion of Modern Investment Treaties' (2014) 58 *International Studies Quarterly* 8.

[133] Williams R 'Nothing Sacred: Developing Countries and the future of International Investment Treaties' available at *http://www.iisd.org/pdf/2011/developing_countries_and_the_future_of_IIAs.pdf* (accessed 20 March 2015).

[134] Mossallam M *Process matters: South Africa's experience exiting its BITs* (GEG working paper, University of Oxford 2015/97) 8.

[135] Woolfrey S 'South Africa's stance on Bilateral Investment Treaties' available at *http://www.tralac.org/discussions/article/5287-south-africa-s-stance-on-bilateral-investment-treaties.html* (accessed on 3 March 2015).

[136] Mossallam M *Process matters: South Africa's experience exiting its BITs* (GEG working paper, University of Oxford 2015/97) 7.

[137] Mossallam M *Process matters: South Africa's experience exiting its BITs* (GEG working paper, University of Oxford 2015/97) 7.

[138] Bernasconi-Osterwalder N & Johnson L 'Commentary to the Austrian Model Investment Treaty' available at *http://media.arbeiterkammer.at/wien/PDF/studien/Studie_Investitionsschutzabkommen_en.pdf* (accessed 20 March 2015).

importing country, South Africa in this case. To date, six of the BITs that South Africa signed using this model template prior to the 21st century have been terminated after a three-year review process of the BITs (hereinafter referred to as the review) that was initiated by the Department of Trade and Industry (DTI) from 2007 -2010.[139]

3.2 Factors that prompted South Africa's BIT review

To provide a better understanding of what prompted South Africa to review its BITs, it is important to begin by providing a brief history of South Africa that led the country to sign its first BIT, the general perspective regarding BITs at the time and the manner in which South Africa entered into its BITs. As was mentioned in the previous section, South Africa entered its first BIT in 1994 soon after attaining its independence. Prior to that, South Africa had no history of negotiating BITs and the risks posed by such treaties were not fully appreciated at that time.[140] South Africa had been undergoing a combination of international sanctions and tight capital controls and, as a result, the country received almost no FDI inflows during apartheid.[141] After independence, South Africa had to reverse the disastrous economic management under apartheid and attracting foreign investment was an important component of the economic strategy.[142] Nelson Mandela was quoted stating that the rates of economic growth could not be achieved without important inflows of foreign capital.[143] He further elaborated that they were determined to create the necessary climate that the foreign investor would find attractive.[144] In working towards achieving this, South Africa had to signal to the world and foreign investors in particular, that it was a safe investment destination.[145] At that time, the

---

[139] UNCTAD 'Speaking notes for workshop on Capital Account Regulations and Global Economic Governance UNCTAD/WTO, Geneva 3-4 October' available at http://unctad.org/meetings/en/Presentation/UNCTAD-GEGI-Carim-2013.pdf (accessed 20 March 2015).

[140] Government Position Paper *Bilateral Investment Treaty Policy Framework Review* (2009) 5.

[141] Poulsen L N S *Sacrificing Sovereignty by Chance: Investment Treaties, Developing Countries and Bounded Rationality* (unpublished Ph.D thesis, London School of Economics and Political Science, 2011) 260.

[142] Poulsen L N S *Sacrificing Sovereignty by Chance: Investment Treaties, Developing Countries and Bounded Rationality* (unpublished Ph.D thesis, London School of Economics and Political Science, 2011) 260.

[143] Nelson Mandela Foundation 'Address by Nelson Mandela at HJ Heinz Company Foundation Distinguished Lecture, Pennsylvania- United States' available at http://www.mandela.gov.za/mandela_speeches/1991/911206_heinz.htm (Accessed 20 March 2015).

[144] Nelson Mandela Foundation 'Address by Nelson Mandela at HJ Heinz Company Foundation Distinguished Lecture, Pennsylvania- United States' available at http://www.mandela.gov.za/mandela_speeches/1991/911206_heinz.htm (Accessed 20 March 2015).

[145] Langalanga A 'South Africa's Foreign Investment Regulation: A Revisit' available at http://blogaila.com/2013/12/05/south-africas-foreign-investment-regulation-a-revisit-by-azwimpheleli-langalanga/ (accessed 20 March 2015).

best way to make a firm signal of such intent was though entering into BITs.[146] Rajan indicates that India entered into its first BIT in 1994 with the UK (the same year in which South Africa ratified its first BIT) and at that time there was a pervasive one-dimensional approach towards BITs that these treaties were instruments aimed at attracting and protecting FDI alone.[147] Under such assumptions, like many other countries during that time, South Africa hastily entered into BITs as a way of attracting FDI.

In addition to reversing the disastrous economic management that was under apartheid, South Africa also had to begin rectifying deeply entrenched racial inequalities that existed prior to South Africa's independence.[148] The new South African government had inherited a society that was among the most unequal in the world, where the vast majority of black South Africans had been excluded from meaningful economic activity under apartheid.[149] As part of a set of initiatives to redress this inheritance and to meet the government's constitutional obligation to create a more open and equitable society based on human rights, black economic empowerment (BEE) programmes were initiated.[150] These programmes were not in line with South Africa's BIT commitments and upon being faced with legal action under the auspices of the ICSID Additional Facility, South Africa initiated a review process of its BITs. The details of the legal issues that arose from the BEE programmes shall be explained below.

The Mineral and Petroleum Resource Development Act of 2004 (MPRDA) is an example of the BEE policies that the South African government implemented. The MPRDA was introduced among other reasons to bring South Africa's mineral rights regime in line with the provisions of its constitution and to provide for the state to fulfil its constitutional role as the custodian of the nation's mineral wealth on behalf of the

---

[146] Langalanga A 'South Africa's Foreign Investment Regulation: A Revisit' available at *http://blogaila.com/2013/12/05/south-africas-foreign-investment-regulation-a-revisit-by-azwimpheleli-langalanga/* (accessed 20 March 2015).
[147] Ranjan P 'India and Bilateral Investment Treaties- A Changing Landscape' (2014) 29 *ICSID Review* 438.
[148] Poulsen L N S *Sacrificing Sovereignty by Chance: Investment Treaties, Developing Countries and Bounded Rationality* (unpublished Ph.D thesis, London School of Economics and Political Science, 2011) 260.
[149]Green AR 'Bilateral investment treaties coming back to bite' available at *http://www.thisisafricaonline.com/Business/Legal-Bulletin/Bilateral-investment-treaties-coming-back-to-bite*(accessed 20 March 2015).
[150]Green AR 'Bilateral investment treaties coming back to bite' available at *http://www.thisisafricaonline.com/Business/Legal-Bulletin/Bilateral-investment-treaties-coming-back-to-bite*(accessed 20 March 2015).

people of South Africa.[151] In 2007, a group of Italian investors who owned granite production companies in South Africa were opposed to the provisions of the MPRDA and South Africa's BEE agenda.[152] The Embassy of Italy in Pretoria submitted an 'Aide Memoire' to the government of South Africa setting forth Italy's view on the BEE legislation and signalling the Italian government's support for the aforementioned Italian investors.[153] Italy warned that the Act might produce a breach of the Italy-South Africa BIT.[154] In particular, Italy warned that the Act's social upliftment objectives and its preferencing of ownership by historically disadvantaged South Africans could be deemed breaches of just, fair and non-discriminatory treatment of Italian nationals.[155] Following these diplomatic interventions, the Italian investors' initiated an arbitration claim against South Africa in terms of the rules of the ICSID Additional Facility in a case that is referred to as the Forestis case.[156] The South African government defended the MPRDA by arguing that it protected existing mineral rights and allowed for their uninterrupted use so long as companies also met the government's wider transformational obligations in the same accepted combination.[157] This was a clear indication of how the South African government was trying to balance its obligations to its foreign investors with the obligations it had to the South African citizens who had been unfairly treated during the apartheid era. Eventually, the case was settled outside the arbitration tribunal following an agreement between the parties whereby South Africa granted the investors new mining rights and the investors requested to discontinue the arbitration

---

[151] Ruff D, Kron J, Golsong C 'Bilateral Investment Treaties in South Africa' available at *http://www.nortonrosefulbright.com/knowledge/publications/118456/bilateral-investment-treaties-in-south-africa* (accessed 20 March 2015).

[152] Canada's Coalition to end Global Poverty 'Bilateral Investment Treaties: A Canadian Primer' available at *http://www.ccic.ca/_files/en/what_we_do/trade_2010-04_investmt_treaties_primer_e.pdf* (accessed 3 March 2015).

[153] Peterson L E & Garland R 'Bilateral Investment Treaties and Land Reform in Southern Africa' 2010 *Rights and Democracy International Centre for Human Rights and Democratic Development*7.

[154] Peterson L E & Garland R 'Bilateral Investment Treaties and Land Reform in Southern Africa' 2010 *Rights and Democracy International Centre for Human Rights and Democratic Development*7.

[155] Peterson L E & Garland R 'Bilateral Investment Treaties and Land Reform in Southern Africa' 2010 *Rights and Democracy International Centre for Human Rights and Democratic Development*7.

[156] Feris J 'Challenging the Status quo- South Africa's termination of its Bilateral Trade Agreements' available at *https://www.dlapiper.com/en/latinamerica/insights/publications/2014/12/international-arbitration-newsletter-q4-2014/challenging-the-status-quo/* (accessed 3 March 2015).

[157]Green AR 'Bilateral investment treaties coming back to bite' available at *http://www.thisisafricaonline.com/Business/Legal-Bulletin/Bilateral-investment-treaties-coming-back-to-bite*(accessed 20 March 2015).

proceedings.[158] Consequently, in 2010 the tribunal dismissed the investors' claims and ordered them to pay part of South Africa's arbitration costs.[159]

Sheffer is of the opinion that the above-mentioned Foresti case could have ended with much weightier consequences for South Africa.[160] The basis of her opinion is the fact that similar cases regarding host-state measures had resulted in tribunals ruling in favour of the foreign investor.[161] Poulsen shared a similar view of the consequences of this case having dire effects on the South African government by indicating that, had the claim by the Italian investors been successful, it had the potential to open the floodgates to similar claims questioning the redistributive efforts of the post-apartheid regime.[162] As a result of this incident, South Africa realised how much BITs were encroaching on its domestic policy space and given the importance of South Africa's social upliftment objectives to the country, the South African government had to rethink its position regarding its BITs.

The Foresti case was not the only indication to South Africa that the BITs encroached on the country's policy space. The first known instance of investors using BITs to promote their interests, vis-à-vis the South African government, was in 2001.[163] During this period South Africa's policy makers suggested a ban on foreign ownership and forced disinvestment among the approximately 5000 private security firms in the country, one of the largest security industries in the world when seen relative to the size of the South African economy.[164] Foreign investors objected fiercely to these suggestions and the British government informed South Africa that any such measure would breach the BIT between the two countries, which would

---

[158] Sheffer M W 'Bilateral Investment Treaties a Friend or Foe of Human Rights?' (2010-2011) 39 *Den. J. Int'l L. & Pol'y 483* 499.
[159] Sheffer M W 'Bilateral Investment Treaties a Friend or Foe of Human Rights?' (2010-2011) 39 *Den. J. Int'l L. & Pol'y 483* 499.
[160] Sheffer M W 'Bilateral Investment Treaties a Friend or Foe of Human Rights?' (2010-2011) 39 *Den. J. Int'l L. & Pol'y 483* 499.
[161] Sheffer M W 'Bilateral Investment Treaties a Friend or Foe of Human Rights?' (2010-2011) 39 *Den. J. Int'l L. & Pol'y 483* 499.
[162] Poulsen L N S *Sacrificing Sovereignty by Chance: Investment Treaties, Developing Countries and Bounded Rationality* (unpublished Ph.D thesis, London School of Economics and Political Science, 2011) 268.
[163] Poulsen L N S *Sacrificing Sovereignty by Chance: Investment Treaties, Developing Countries and Bounded Rationality* (unpublished Ph.D thesis, London School of Economics and Political Science, 2011) 263.
[164] Poulsen L N S *Sacrificing Sovereignty by Chance: Investment Treaties, Developing Countries and Bounded Rationality* (unpublished Ph.D thesis, London School of Economics and Political Science, 2011) 263.

result in legal recourse for the British citizens.[165] Eventually, the foreign-owned security companies won the argument.[166] Kicking out firms who brought in close to two billion Rands a year turned out to be too costly an endeavour for the South African government even without a BIT claim.[167] From this experience, South Africa began to realise the limitation that was placed on the government's policy space by its commitment to BITs. This incident, together with that of the Foresti case gave South Africa a practical experience of the effect that BITs have on domestic policy space and as such contributed to the country rethinking its position regarding BITs.

In 2004, prior to the Foresti case, South Africa was called upon to respond to investor claims based on BIT provisions. A Swiss investor who had acquired a game reserve that was later subject to poaching, vandalism and theft initiated the claims.[168] The investor alleged, among many other allegations, that the government had failed in its treaty obligations to provide protection and security.[169] The tribunal found South Africa in breach of its obligations to provide full protection and security and it awarded the investor almost seven million Rands in compensation, which the South African government paid a year later.[170] Having suffered a non-trivial loss in compensating the investor, South Africa began to realise the legal and practical implications of its BITs and the harsh consequences of failure to adhere to BIT provisions. As such, South Africa had to evaluate the risks and benefits from such treaties and come up with measures that would avoid facing such similar cases in the future.

Another situation that triggered the review of South Africa's BITs was the development that South Africa was undergoing from the time of signing its first BIT to the modern day South Africa. South Africa's first model BIT, which was the basis for

---

[165] Poulsen L N S *Sacrificing Sovereignty by Chance: Investment Treaties, Developing Countries and Bounded Rationality* (unpublished Ph.D thesis, London School of Economics and Political Science, 2011) 263.
[166] Poulsen L N S *Sacrificing Sovereignty by Chance: Investment Treaties, Developing Countries and Bounded Rationality* (unpublished Ph.D thesis, London School of Economics and Political Science, 2011) 264.
[167] Poulsen L N S *Sacrificing Sovereignty by Chance: Investment Treaties, Developing Countries and Bounded Rationality* (unpublished Ph.D thesis, London School of Economics and Political Science, 2011) 264.
[168] Lang J 'Bilateral Investment Treaties- a shield or a sword?' available at *http://www.bowman.co.za/FileBrowser/ArticleDocuments/South-African-Government-Canceling-Bilateral-Investment-Treaties.pdf* (accessed 20 March 2015).
[169] Lang J 'Bilateral Investment Treaties- a shield or a sword?' available at *http://www.bowman.co.za/FileBrowser/ArticleDocuments/South-African-Government-Canceling-Bilateral-Investment-Treaties.pdf* (accessed 20 March 2015).
[170] Poulsen L N S *Sacrificing Sovereignty by Chance: Investment Treaties, Developing Countries and Bounded Rationality* (unpublished Ph.D thesis, London School of Economics and Political Science, 2011) 265.

concluding all subsequent BITs, was negotiated or entered into before the adoption of the new constitution in 1996.[171] This constitution provides robust safeguards to protect private property and investments in the country.[172] Examples of such safeguards are evident in section 25 of the Constitution of South Africa that provides protection for property rights and section 9 that prohibits discrimination on various grounds. The horizontal protection established in this constitution and South Africa's legislation is complemented by sectoral regimes that cover among other things finance, banking, communication and mining.[173] Moreover, apart from the developments in South Africa's legislation, the country developed to rank amongst the most open jurisdictions in the world, providing investment protection through domestic law that is consistent with the highest international standards.[174] Such developments countered the use of BITs in protecting foreign investments in South Africa and with such developments, South Africa had to rethink its position regarding the use of BITs.

To add to how South Africa's development contributed to the review process, Gordon and Pohl indicate that each investment treaty reflects a specific approach to protecting covered investors and managing legal risks for treaty partners.[175] As the distinction between capital exporting and capital importing countries continues to fade, many countries would be classified as being in both categories and countries' perceived self-interests in relation to investment treaties may have evolved.[176] Investment protection may gain in importance for countries with emerging capital export activities while management of legal risks may assume greater importance to countries that have traditionally been capital exporters but now receive significant

[171] UNCTAD 'Speaking notes for workshop on Capital Account Regulations and Global Economic Governance UNCTAD/WTO, Geneva 3-4 October' available at *http://unctad.org/meetings/en/Presentation/UNCTAD-GEGI-Carim-2013.pdf* (accessed 20 March 2015).

[172] UNCTAD 'Speaking notes for workshop on Capital Account Regulations and Global Economic Governance UNCTAD/WTO, Geneva 3-4 October' available at *http://unctad.org/meetings/en/Presentation/UNCTAD-GEGI-Carim-2013.pdf* (accessed 20 March 2015).

[173] Carrim X 'Lessons from South Africa's Bilateral Investment Treaties Review' available at *http://ccsi.columbia.edu/files/2013/10/No 109 - Carim - FINAL.pdf* (accessed 20 March, 2015).

[174] Carrim X 'Lessons from South Africa's Bilateral Investment Treaties Review' available at *http://ccsi.columbia.edu/files/2013/10/No 109 - Carim - FINAL.pdf* (accessed 20 March, 2015).

[175] Gordon K &Pohl J 'Investment Treaties Over Time- Treaty Practice and Interpretation in a Changing World' 2015/02 *OECD* 9.

[176] Gordon K &Pohl J 'Investment Treaties Over Time- Treaty Practice and Interpretation in a Changing World' 2015/02 *OECD*9.

capital inflows.[177] Johnson elaborates on this same view by indicating that countries need specific BIT provisions depending on their progressive stages of development.[178] These provisions would help the countries keep up with their economic development agenda.[179] As Randal points out, South Africa developed from a capital importing country to a capital exporting country with the levels of domestic investment increasing[180] and as such, the provisions in South Africa's earlier BITs no longer served important needs for the South African government. South Africa's focus had shifted from not only protecting foreign investments but also protecting and promoting its local investors and equating the conditions in which investors were treated among other factors. Such developments further necessitated that South Africa rethink its position regarding BITs.

The international trend regarding BITs also had a bearing on South Africa's decision to review its BITs. De Gama points out that South Africa observed the fractious debate in the OECD over a multilateral investment agreement.[181] From this, South Africa gained insight into the issues that other countries were experiencing with their BITs. South Africa also participated in the discussions in the WTO that sought to include investment as one of the Singapore Issues in the Doha Round negotiations.[182] South Africa's involvement in both these events provided an awakening regarding issues related to BITs from other countries experiences. The rise in international investment arbitrations that followed the financial crisis of 2001 further contributed to South Africa's knowledge of the risks that were associated with

---

[177] Gordon K &Pohl J 'Investment Treaties Over Time- Treaty Practice and Interpretation in a Changing World' 2015/02 *OECD*9.

[178] Johnson A R 'Rethinking Bilateral Investment Treaties for Sub-Saharan Africa'(2009-2010) 59 *Emory L. J. 919* 922.

[179] Johnson A R 'Rethinking Bilateral Investment Treaties for Sub-Saharan Africa'(2009-2010) 59 *Emory L. J. 919* 922.

[180] Williams R 'Nothing Sacred: Developing Countries and the future of International Investment Treaties' available at *http://www.iisd.org/pdf/2011/developing_countries_and_the_future_of_IIAs.pdf* (accessed 20 March 2015).

[181] De Gama M M 'South Africa's Promotion and Protection of Investment Bill' available at *www.saiia.org.za%2Fdoc_download%2F688-2015-02-16-fdi-presentation-dr-mustaqeem-de-gama* (accessed 20 March 2015).

[182] Mossallam M *Process matters: South Africa's experience exiting its BITs* (GEG working paper, University of Oxford 2015/97) 9.

the BITs.[183] This, in addition to South Africa's own experiences as being respondent to ICSID cases, all contributed to South Africa rethinking its position regarding BITs.

In their proposition for BIT renegotiation, Haftel and Thompson indicate that BIT negotiators lacked information when they consummated the original agreements and that governments were able to update over time, meaning to say that learning took place.[184] This proposition seems true for the South African government that learnt not only from its personal experience of being a respondent to BIT claims but also from the knowledge it acquired from arbitrations between other countries. The UNCTAD Issue Notes indicate that since the year 2000, there has been a marked increase in arbitrations under BITs worldwide.[185] The awards in these cases have shown evidence of inconsistencies.[186] There are divergent legal interpretations of identical or similar provisions and differences in the assessment of the merits of the cases involving the same facts.[187] To further complicate this fragmented system is the fact that there is the absence of an appellate process which often falls short of meeting the standards of legal correctness and consistency.[188] Under Article 52 (4) of the ICSID Additional Facility rules, awards given shall be final and binding on the parties. The growing number of cases and the inconsistencies mentioned, which are not subject to appeal, have led to uncertainty about the meaning of treaty obligations leading to the unpredictability of how the treaties are interpreted.[189] All this became apparent to South Africa after it had entered into its BITs. Being a signatory to such treaty provisions became a cause of concern for the South African government contributing to the decision by South Africa to review its BIT policy framework.

---

[183] Mossallam M *Process matters: South Africa's experience exiting its BITs* (GEG working paper, University of Oxford 2015/97) 9.
[184]Haftel Y & Thompson A *When Do States Renegotiate International Agreements? The Case of Bilateral Investment Treaties* (working paper, University of Maryland 2013) 7.
[185] UNCTAD 'Recent developments in investor-state disputes ISDS' Issue note number 1 May 2013 available at *http://unctad.org/en/publicationslibrary/webdiaepcb2013d3_en.pdf*(accessed 20 March 2015).
[186] Carrim X 'South Africa and Bilateral Investment Treaties' available at *www.thetradebeat.com%2Fdoc_download%2F17-south-africa-and-bilateral-investment-treaties* (accessed 20 March 2015).
[187] UNCTAD 'Speaking notes for workshop on Capital Account Regulations and Global Economic Governance UNCTAD/WTO, Geneva 3-4 October' available at *http://unctad.org/meetings/en/Presentation/UNCTAD-GEGI-Carim-2013.pdf* (accessed 20 March 2015).
[188] Carrim X 'Lessons from South Africa's Bilateral Investment Treaties Review' available at *http://ccsi.columbia.edu/files/2013/10/No_109_-_Carim_-_FINAL.pdf* (accessed 20 March, 2015).
[189] Carrim X 'South Africa and Bilateral Investment Treaties' available at *www.thetradebeat.com%2Fdoc_download%2F17-south-africa-and-bilateral-investment-treaties* (accessed 20 March 2015).

Moreover, South Africa also learnt that the growing number of cases was challenging government measures such as changes to the domestic regulatory framework, the tax regime, public tenders, public health, the environment and measures that were aimed to address the financial crisis bailouts and withdrawal of subsidies.[190] In these cases, 75 percent of the awards were in favour of foreign investors and significantly high arbitration costs were involved with such disputes (more than US$ 8 million on average per case).[191] Such situations are undesirable for any country with BITs and too harsh to be ignored. To worsen the situation, the arbitration process includes three individuals that are appointed on an ad hoc basis who access acts of states, in particular, sensitive public policy issues that undermine countries' domestic legal systems.[192] Such observations on international trends regarding BITs also contributed to South Africa's decision to review its BITs.

A public statement by South Africa's trade minister reveals that the government justified their decisions to update their investment protection regime as being consistent with global trends.[193] Such trends include the fact that Latin American governments have come out strongly in opposition to prevailing norms resulting in Bolivia, Ecuador, and Venezuela denouncing the ICSID while India and Mexico have both refused to be party to the ICSID.[194] Brazil has not ratified any of its BITs.[195] There has also been a considerable re-writing of BITs in countries such as the United States and Canada to mention a few.[196] The European Union and India are

---

[190] Carrim X 'South Africa and Bilateral Investment Treaties' available at *www.thetradebeat.com%2Fdoc_download%2F17-south-africa-and-bilateral-investment-treaties* (accessed 20 March 2015).

[191] Carrim X 'South Africa and Bilateral Investment Treaties' available at *www.thetradebeat.com%2Fdoc_download%2F17-south-africa-and-bilateral-investment-treaties* (accessed 20 March 2015).

[192] Carrim X 'South Africa and Bilateral Investment Treaties' available at *www.thetradebeat.com%2Fdoc_download%2F17-south-africa-and-bilateral-investment-treaties* (accessed 20 March 2015).

[193] Mossallam M *Process matters: South Africa's experience exiting its BITs* (GEG working paper, University of Oxford 2015/97) 10.

[194] Green AR 'Bilateral investment treaties coming back to bite' available at *http://www.thisisafricaonline.com/Business/Legal-Bulletin/Bilateral-investment-treaties-coming-back-to-bite*(accessed 20 March 2014).

[195] Green AR 'Bilateral investment treaties coming back to bite' available at *http://www.thisisafricaonline.com/Business/Legal-Bulletin/Bilateral-investment-treaties-coming-back-to-bite*(accessed 20 March 2014).

[196] Carrim X 'South Africa and Bilateral Investment Treaties' available at *www.thetradebeat.com%2Fdoc_download%2F17-south-africa-and-bilateral-investment-treaties* (accessed 20 March 2015).

also in the process of reviewing their BITs.[197] Gordon and Pohl indicate that in a sample of countries that had brought their IIAs in force since 1959, at least 170 treaties or at least nine percent of the sub-sample had been amended, complemented after signature by protocols, replaced, denounced or ended by mutual agreement.[198] New approaches to investment treaties are emerging to mitigate risks of earlier agreements through more precise drafting of provisions.[199] As such, South Africa had to keep up with global trends regarding BITs.

There are also other factors that contributed to South Africa reviewing its BITs that shall be briefly indicated. Mossallam points out that at the time the decision to review was made, most of South Africa's BITs were about to reach their renewal phases.[200] This required South Africa to take immediate action in revising their BITs. South Africa was also realising that it was getting FDI from countries that did not have BITs with South Africa, which also prompted South Africa to rethink its position regarding BITs. Williams also points out that he had requested that the South African government consider revisiting its BITs after he had investigated what South Africa had signed up for in its earlier BIT commitments.[201] William's request was however not taken up immediately due to the lack of coordination of South Africa's BIT policy at the time, that saw continued negotiations of BITs despite the imposition of a moratorium.[202] All these factors indicated above contributed to the decision to review South Africa's BITs.

---

[197] Carrim X 'South Africa and Bilateral Investment Treaties' available at www.thetradebeat.com%2Fdoc_download%2F17-south-africa-and-bilateral-investment-treaties (accessed 20 March 2015).

[198] Gordon K &Pohl J 'Investment Treaties Over Time- Treaty Practice and Interpretation in a Changing World' 2015/02 *OECD* 17.

[199] Carrim X 'South Africa and Bilateral Investment Treaties' available at www.thetradebeat.com%2Fdoc_download%2F17-south-africa-and-bilateral-investment-treaties (accessed 20 March 2015).

[200] Mossallam M *Process matters: South Africa's experience exiting its BITs* (GEG working paper, University of Oxford 2015/97) 10.

[201] Williams R 'Nothing Sacred: Developing Countries and the future of International Investment Treaties' available at http://www.iisd.org/pdf/2011/developing_countries_and_the_future_of_IIAs.pdf (accessed 20 March 2015).

[202] Poulsen L N S 'Bounded Rationality and the Diffusion of Modern Investment Treaties' (2014) 58 *International Studies Quarterly* 11.

3.3 South Africa's BIT review process

South Africa's BIT review process does not differ substantially from other nations that have undertaken BIT reviews. Countries that have reviewed their treaties such as the United States, Canada, Norway, Sweden had, among other factors, targeted the review mechanism to specific aspects. The United States, for example, revisited its model BIT with emphasis on three aspects; the dispute settlement provisions, the state-owned enterprises and financial services issues.[203] South Africa's review process was however targeted at assessing the role of foreign investment in the country, the levels of protection afforded to investment, and the risks and benefits of BITs.[204] In addition, as part of the review process, the South African Department of Trade and Industry (DTI) was mandated to review and strengthen the country's investment regime in order to open the country up to FDI, while still maintaining the sovereign right to pursue policy objectives.[205]

With the aforementioned objectives and mandates in mind, the DTI invited the participation of various stakeholders that included businesses, labour, government, local and international institutions.[206] This was also akin to the method that was used by the United States in its review process since it also considered the views of an advisory committee composed of a diverse group of investment experts, representing the businesses, academia, labour, environmental NGOs and legal professions.[207] The participation of various local stakeholders in South Africa was achieved through detailed interviews at the management level with the DTI.[208] South

---

[203] Vis-Dunbar D 'Advisory Committee Submits report on the United States Model Bilateral Investment Treaty' available at http://www.iisd.org/itn/2009/10/01/advisory-committee-submits-report-on-the-united-states-model-bilateral-investment-treaty/ (accessed 20 March 2015).

[204] Carrim X 'Lessons from South Africa`s Bilateral Investment Treaties Review' available at http://ccsi.columbia.edu/files/2013/10/No_109 - Carim - FINAL.pdf (accessed 4 March, 2015).

[205] Masamba M 'Africa and Bilateral Investment Treaties: to "BIT"or Not' available at http://www.consultancyafrica.com/index.php?option=com_content&view=article&id=1697:africa-and-bilateral-investment-treaties-to-bit-or-not&catid=82:african-industry-a-business&Itemid=266 (accessed 4 March 2015).

[206] Government Position Paper *Bilateral Investment Treaty Policy Framework Review* (2009) 6.

[207] Anderson S 'The New U.S Model Bilateral Investment Treaty: A Public Interest Critique' available at http://www.ips-dc.org/the_new_us_model_bilateral_investment_treaty_a_public_interest_critique/(accessed 4 March 2015).

[208] Government Position Paper *Bilateral Investment Treaty Policy Framework Review* (2009) 6.

Africa went further by conducting meetings regarding the review outside of South Africa at UNCTAD and the South Centre.[209]

The BIT review process included three drafts, the first of which was an initial policy document based on research collected through interviewing the bilateral units in the international trade division who directly worked with BITs.[210] This also included an internal government workshop that brought policy makers together to discuss the results of the review and receive feedback on it.[211] The second draft of the policy paper encompassed the feedback from the first draft and was published online as well as in the newspapers for public comment.[212] The feedback received from this draft was integrated into the third draft that was sent to the cabinet.[213] It is important to note that in 2010, at the completion of the review process, the South African government published the key findings of the review and the measures South Africa was planning to take as determined by the cabinet.[214]

The review process that South Africa undertook will be assessed further in this chapter with specific focus centered on the target areas that South Africa considered when it reviewed its BITs. Although the factors that were alluded to earlier include the role of foreign investment in South Africa, the level of protection afforded to investment and the risks and benefits of BITs, most of the focus shall be centered on the risks that were inherent in South Africa's BITs that were evident during the review process. However, brief highlights on the factors that helped conclude the role of foreign investment in the context of BITs and the evaluation of protection that was afforded to investment in South Africa by South Africa's BITs shall also be indicated so as to provide a better understanding of the outcome of the review process.

---

[209] Mossallam M *Process matters: South Africa's experience exiting its BITs* (GEG working paper, University of Oxford 2015/97) 21.

[210] Mossallam M *Process matters: South Africa's experience exiting its BITs* (GEG working paper, University of Oxford 2015/97) 11.

[211] Williams R 'Nothing Sacred: Developing Countries and the future of International Investment Treaties' available at http://www.iisd.org/pdf/2011/developing_countries_and_the_future_of_IIAs.pdf (accessed 3 March 2015).

[212] Government Position Paper*Bilateral Investment Treaty Policy Framework Review* (2009) 13.

[213] Mossallam M *Process matters: South Africa's experience exiting its BITs* (GEG working paper, University of Oxford 2015/97) 12.

[214] Mossallam M *Process matters: South Africa's experience exiting its BITs* (GEG working paper, University of Oxford 2015/97) 21.

3.3.1 Risks inherent in South Africa's BITs

The risks that were inherent in South Africa's BITs were evident from an analysis that was conducted on the individual BITs with reference to the prevailing BIT arbitrations, the current trends regarding BITs and how other countries were treating their BITs. The analysis was also carried out with the objective of establishing how the BITs co-existed with South Africa's domestic legislative framework. South Africa analysed its BITs based on 11 standard clauses that are found in South Africa's BITs.[215] This chapter will focus on a few of these standard clauses with regards to their interpretation and in the context of South Africa's domestic legislative framework.

3.3.1.1 Individual analysis based on interpretation of the provisions

South Africa's BITs provide for a definition of terms. Some of the terms are broadly defined in the treaties. The term investment for example is defined in Article 1 of the BITs that South Africa signed with Germany, Netherlands, UK and Korea, to mention a few as 'any kind of asset invested by the investor of one contracting party'. The definition in some of these treaties goes further to highlight certain assets considered as an investment and indicating that the list was not exclusive. As was explained in section 2.2 of the previous chapter, such a definition would lead to an interpretation that would include assets that are not acquired for economic benefits or business purposes. Such interpretations could lead to claims from property that South Africa had not considered as investments in its treaties. This thereby served as an indication that such definitions had to be narrowed down in order to cover only the aspects desired by the South African government.

The fair and equitable treatment provision in South Africa's BITs was also examined and concluded as being too broad and vague.[216] It was also highlighted during the review how such a provision had been subject to inconsistent interpretations by

[215]Government Position Paper *Bilateral Investment Treaty Policy Framework Review* (2009) 8.
[216]Woolfrey S 'South Africa's Promotion and Protection of Investment Bill' available at *http://www.tralac.org/discussions/article/5345-south-africa-s-promotion-and-protection-of-investment-bill.html*(accessed 4 March 2015).

international arbitration tribunals in other disputes.[217] The fair and equitable provision is phrased similarly in most of South Africa's BITs and provides that,

> 'investments of nationals or companies of each contracting party shall at all times be accorded fair and equitable treatment and shall enjoy full protection and security in the territory of the other contracting party.'[218]

The analysis revealed that such a provision potentially allows foreign investors to seek compensation if the conditions under which their investment was made (including any applicable domestic regulations) are later changed in ways detrimental to the investor's interests.[219] This would result in potential legal disputes at international tribunals that would be costly for the South African Government, as was evident in the Foresti case, and that of the Swiss investor indicated above.

Another risk that was indicated in South Africa's review process was found in the investor-state arbitration clause found in most of South Africa's BITs. As was explained in the previous chapter, this provision allows investors to sue states based on measures that the investors deem to have violated the respective BITs that would be protecting the investors. This indicated to the South African government that the provision could allow foreign investors to challenge domestic public interest laws and measures in front of ad hoc international arbitral tribunals if such measures were deemed to have violated the investors BIT rights.[220] As was evident in the Foresti case, this would not only affect the government's ability to make changes to its domestic law for public interest but would also undermine the functions and duties of the legislature and the judiciary system of the country. It would also affect the sovereignty of the host state being sued at international tribunals. Moreover, the high costs of defending such challenges against the government would be unwarranted.

---

[217]Woolfrey S 'South Africa's Promotion and Protection of Investment Bill' available at *http://www.tralac.org/discussions/article/5345-south-africa-s-promotion-and-protection-of-investment-bill.html*(accessed 4 March 2015).

[218]Agreement between the Government of the United Kingdom of Great Britain and Northern Ireland and the Government of the Republic of South Africa. Treaty Series No.35 (1998) Article 2.

[219]Woolfrey S 'South Africa's Promotion and Protection of Investment Bill' available at *http://www.tralac.org/discussions/article/5345-south-africa-s-promotion-and-protection-of-investment-bill.html*(accessed 4 March 2015).

[220]Lang J 'Bilateral Investment Treaties- a shield or a sword?' available at *http://www.bowman.co.za/FileBrowser/ArticleDocuments/South-African-Government-Canceling-Bilateral-Investment-Treaties.pdf* (accessed 4 March 2015).

An analysis of the overall BIT structure indicated that the BITs placed all the obligations on the host state and awarded all the rights to the investors.[221] South Africa was mostly a capital importing country at the conclusion of its first BITs soon after its independence and was obliged to promote and protect investors' investment, to treat all its investors equally, to compensate investors for any losses suffered as a result of wars or any such kind of mishaps, to guide against expropriations or nationalising investors assets and even allowing for free transfer of funds. Such obligations on the state would be entitlements to the foreign investors. An example of a BIT in which all this is highlighted is that of the South Africa-UK BIT.[222]

3.3.1.2 Analysis of South Africa's review process in the context of its domestic legislative framework

The national treatment provision that is contained in South Africa's BITs was examined in the context of South Africa's legislative framework. The purpose of the national treatment provision is to protect foreign investors from laws and regulations or government policy that may treat domestic investors more favourably than them.[223] South Africa's BITs differ markedly in terms of their national treatment commitments.[224] For example, the South Africa - Netherlands BIT in Article 3(2) provides that

> 'each contracting party shall accord to such investments treatment which in any case shall not be less favourable than that which it accords to investments of its own investors or to investments of investors of any third State, whichever is more favourable to the investor concerned.'

The South Africa - Tanzania BIT however, goes further in elaborating that the national treatment provision

---

[221] Williams R 'Nothing Sacred: Developing Countries and the future of International Investment Treaties' available at *http://www.iisd.org/pdf/2011/developing_countries_and_the_future_of_IIAs.pdf* (accessed 3 March 2015).

[222] Agreement between the Government of the United Kingdom of Great Britain and Northern Ireland and the Government of the Republic of South Africa. Treaty Series No.35 (1998).

[223] Lang J 'Bilateral Investment Treaties- a shield or a sword?' available at *http://www.bowman.co.za/FileBrowser/ArticleDocuments/South-African-Government-Canceling-Bilateral-Investment-Treaties.pdf* (accessed 4 March 2015).

[224] Peterson L 'South Africa's Bilateral Investment Treaties Implications for Development and Human Rights'(2006) 6 *Dialogue on Globalisation Occasional Paper* 29.

'shall not be construed so as to oblige one party to extend to the investors of the other Party the benefit of any treatment, preference or privilege resulting from ...any law or other measure the purpose of which is to promote the achievement of equality in its territory, or designed to protect or advance persons, or categories of persons, disadvantaged by unfair discrimination in its territory.'

The phrasing of the Netherlands BIT, and others like it, does not include any reference to the rights of governments to accord preferential treatment to locals in certain circumstances.[225] This directly contradicts section 9 (2) of the Constitution of South Africa of 2006, which provides for affirmative action measures. Such measures are designed to protect or advance persons or categories of persons, disadvantaged by unfair discrimination so as to promote the achievement of equality.[226] The phrasing of the Netherlands BIT hinders the application of this constitutional provision since it prohibits any form of discrimination regardless of the basis for such a measure.

In addition, the national treatment provisions found in South Africa's BITs affected the Broad-Based Black Economic Empowerment Act 53 of 2003 (B-BBEEA). The preamble of the Act states that, among other factors, the Act aims to promote the achievement of the constitutional right to equality, increase broad-based and effective participation of black people in the economy and promote a higher growth rate, increased employment and more equitable income distribution amongst the South African People. The preamble also provides for the establishment of a national policy on broad-based black economic empowerment. The result has been the BEE policy that was briefly discussed earlier in this chapter that lays down the objectives that the government has to meet in order to achieve the purpose of the B-BBEEA.[227] Among the policy objectives include the achievement of a substantial change in the racial composition of ownership and management structures and in the skilled

[225] Khisa I 'Talks on EAC-US trade, investment deal face hurdles' available at http://www.theeastafrican.co.ke/business/-investment-deal-face-hurdles/-/2560/2451498/-/item/0/-/qfferbz/-/index.html (accessed 4 March 2015).

[226] Klaaren J & Schneiderman D *Investor-State Arbitration and South Africa's Bilateral Investment Treaty Policy Framework Review* (comment submitted to the DTI, Mandela Institute 2009) 4.

[227] South Africa Info 'Black Economic Empowerment' available at http://www.southafrica.info/business/trends/empowerment/bee.htm#.VP8F78s5DIU#ixzz3Tzozbky6 (accessed 3 March 2015).

occupations of existing and new enterprises.[228] It became apparent during the review process that the provisions of this policy were problematic in that foreign-owned firms could argue that obligations to hire a certain percentage of black managers over a certain period of time, or the obligation to acquire BEE equity partners served to discriminate against foreign-owned business on a de facto basis because black-owned firms would have met such obligations already.[229] With this revelation and the experience in responding to the Foresti case, South Africa had to take measures to avoid the impact of responding to more cases at international arbitration for violating its BIT provisions through its domestic policies.

The above mentioned result of the review with regards to preferential policies violating national treatment provisions also further highlighted that the government would also be limited in applying other preferential government policies or schemes such as subsidies, grants or other forms of special treatment provided to local cultural industries such as film or television production.[230] Such treatment might be construed by foreign-owned enterprises as providing more favourable treatment to locals contrary to South Africa's investment treaty obligations.[231] This clearly indicated that South Africa was limited from forming new policies that could have been beneficial to its country based on its commitments to the BITs that it had signed in the previous century.

South Africa's BITs also prohibit nationalisation or expropriation of foreign investments. Article 4 (2) of the Germany BIT provides that

> 'investments by nationals or companies of either contracting party shall not be expropriated, nationalised or subjected to any other measure the effects of which would be tantamount to expropriation or nationalisation in the territory of the other contracting party except for the public interest and against compensation.'

---

[228] South Africa Info 'Black Economic Empowerment' available at *http://www.southafrica.info/business/trends/empowerment/bee.htm#.VP8F78s5DIU#ixzz3Tzozbky6* (accessed 3 March 2015).

[229] South Africa Info 'Black Economic Empowerment' available at *http://www.southafrica.info/business/trends/empowerment/bee.htm#.VP8F78s5DIU#ixzz3Tzozbky6* (accessed 3 March 2015).

[230] Peterson L 'South Africa's Bilateral Investment Treaties Implications for Development and Human Rights'(2006) 6 *Dialogue on Globalisation Occasional Paper* 32.

[231] Peterson L 'South Africa's Bilateral Investment Treaties Implications for Development and Human Rights'(2006) 6 *Dialogue on Globalisation Occasional Paper* 32.

From the phrasing of this article, it is evident that the provision relates to any measure that impacts the use of property and deprives investors of expected economic benefit.[232] This provision and others phrased similarly in South Africa's BITs do not distinguish between expropriation and deprivation implying that deprivation would be tantamount to expropriation and would result in compensation.[233] South Africa's constitution, however, clearly stipulates in section 25 that deprivation would not require compensation if the measures were pursuant to law and not arbitrary. This indicated another problem area that was inherent in South Africa's BITs.

Further evidence of the undesirable consequences of phrasing the expropriation clause broadly as in the Germany BIT may be shown by the conclusions drawn by the governments of Canada and the United States. These conclusions are important in the discussion of South Africa's review process because the conclusions were based on a ruling that indicated that deprivation in whole or significant part would constitute an expropriation contrary to the treaty no matter the purpose underlying that deprivation.[234] Canada and the United States concluded that it could be dangerous to leave it to arbitrators to draw the line between legitimate government regulation and compensable expropriations.[235] These conclusions were drawn from the North American Free Trade Agreement (NAFTA) Chapter 11 investment arbitration involving *Metalclad v. Mexico*.[236] In this case, the arbitral tribunal ruled that,

> 'expropriation could be defined broadly, so as to include not only literal seizure or destruction of property, but also covert or incidental interference with the use of property which has the effect of depriving the owner, in whole

[232] Carrim X 'South Africa and Bilateral Investment Treaties' available at *www.thetradebeat.com%2Fdoc_download%2F17-south-africa-and-bilateral-investment-treaties* (accessed 4 March 2015).

[233] Mossallam M *Process matters: South Africa's experience exiting its BITs* (GEG working paper, University of Oxford 2015/97) 8.

[234] Peterson L 'South Africa's Bilateral Investment Treaties Implications for Development and Human Rights' (2006)6 *Dialogue on Globalisation Occasional Paper* 22.

[235] Peterson L 'South Africa's Bilateral Investment Treaties Implications for Development and Human Rights' (2006)6 *Dialogue on Globalisation Occasional Paper* 23.

[236] Peterson L 'South Africa's Bilateral Investment Treaties Implications for Development and Human Rights' (2006)6 *Dialogue on Globalisation Occasional Paper* 23.

or significant part, of the use or reasonably-to-be-expected economic benefit of property.'[237]

This further indicates how the South African BITs posed a risk of adverse effects drawn from the interpretation of the provisions that South Africa entered into.

South Africa's BITs further violated the country's constitution in the provisions relating to the calculation of compensation. The measure of compensation provided for under the constitution of South Africa differs from and affords less protection than that provided under South Africa's BITs.[238] South Africa's BITs use language such as genuine value, actual value, real value and market value, terms that are all generally understood to import a concept akin to market value.[239] The constitution, however, provides for compensation to be just and equitable, reflecting on equitable balance between the public interest and the interests of those affected, having regard to all relevant circumstances.[240] The public interest is expressly stated to indicate the nation's commitment to land reform and to reforms to bring about equitable access to all of South Africa's natural resources, a methodology which is more likely to provide compensation at less than market value.[241]

Over and above the constitutional provisions that were being violated by the BITs that South Africa had signed, the MPRDA was also a violation of certain BIT provisions as the Italian investors pointed out to South Africa. The aim of the Act is to promote greater participation of blacks and racial equity in the South African mining sector through, for example, setting minimum criteria for black ownership and management. [242] This, for example, included the requirement for mining companies

[237]Peterson L 'South Africa's Bilateral Investment Treaties Implications for Development and Human Rights' (2006)6 *Dialogue on Globalisation Occasional Paper* 23.
[238] Mossallam M *Process matters: South Africa's experience exiting its BITs* (GEG working paper, University of Oxford 2015/97) 24.
[239]Lang J 'Bilateral Investment Treaties- a shield or a sword?' available at *http://www.bowman.co.za/FileBrowser/ArticleDocuments/South-African-Government-Canceling-Bilateral-Investment-Treaties.pdf* (accessed 4 March 2015).
[240] Constitution of the Republic of South Africa 108 of 1996 section 25 (3).
[241]Lang J 'Bilateral Investment Treaties- a shield or a sword?' available at *http://www.bowman.co.za/FileBrowser/ArticleDocuments/South-African-Government-Canceling-Bilateral-Investment-Treaties.pdf* (accessed 4 March 2015).
[242]Canada's Coalition to end Global Poverty 'Bilateral Investment Treaties: A Canadian Primer' available at*http://www.ccic.ca/_files/en/what_we_do/trade_2010-04_investmt_treaties_primer_e.pdf* (accessed 3 March 2015).

to transfer 26 percent of their shares to historically disadvantaged South Africans.[243] Not only would this be regarded as a breach of the national treatment provision, but also that of expropriation by foreign investors.[244] This thereby made it clear to the South African authorities that the ability of the state to regulate its domestic public policy objectives was under serious threat from their BIT obligations.

3.3.2 The role of BITs in attracting foreign investment in South Africa

Developing countries have traditionally regarded the availability of a BIT as a means of attracting FDI. With this view in mind, countries such as South Africa in the period soon after it attained its independence, signed many BITs with developed countries in the hopes of attracting FDI. In reviewing the role that the BITs played in attracting FDI, the South African government considered international reports on studies that were aimed at establishing the same. Such reports authored by the World Bank and UNCTAD, amongst others, indicated that there was no clear relationship between BITs and increased FDI inflows.[245] The UNCTAD report clearly stated that BITs are relatively insignificant in determining amounts of FDI.[246] The study further indicated that other factors such as market size and growth, exchange rate and country risks appeared to determine FDI more strongly.[247]

The process of the review with regards to the role of BITs in attracting FDI also looked at examples of other countries. Brazil, for example, is considered as one of the largest magnets for inward FDI in Latin America and yet Brazil has not ratified any of the BITs that it has signed.[248] In comparison, South Africa has BITs in force

[243]Columbia Centre on Sustainable Investment 'Local Content South Africa- Mining & Petroleum' available at *http://ccsi.columbia.edu/files/2014/03/Local-Content-South-Africa-Mining-and-Petroleum-CCSI-Feb-2015.pdf* (accessed 5 March 2015).

[244] Investment Treaty News 'South Africa begins withdrawing from EU-member BITs' available at *http://www.iisd.org/itn/2012/10/30/news-in-brief-9/* (accessed 5 March 2015).

[245]Carrim X 'South Africa and Bilateral Investment Treaties' available at *www.thetradebeat.com%2Fdoc_download%2F17-south-africa-and-bilateral-investment-treaties* (accessed 4 March 2015).

[246]Klaaren J & Schneiderman D *Investor-State Arbitration and South Africa's Bilateral Investment Treaty Policy Framework Review* (comment submitted to the DTI, Mandela Institute 2009) 6.

[247]Klaaren J & Schneiderman D *Investor-State Arbitration and South Africa's Bilateral Investment Treaty Policy Framework Review* (comment submitted to the DTI, Mandela Institute 2009) 6.

[248]Klaaren J & Schneiderman D *Investor-State Arbitration and South Africa's Bilateral Investment Treaty Policy Framework Review* (comment submitted to the DTI, Mandela Institute 2009) 6.

but receives no FDI from many countries with whom they have BITs.[249] Large investments that came into South Africa were from non-treaty partners that included the US, India, Malaysia and Brazil.[250]

Furthermore, a study undertaken by a private consulting firm in South Africa found that foreign investments only ranked legal certainty as the eighth determinant in the decision whether to invest in South Africa or not.[251] The most important determinate was considered to be market size.[252] Williams expressed the view that when developed countries sign BITs, they seek only to address one determinate of FDI, which is legal certainty that is meant to protect the investment and not attract FDI.[253] The South African constitution that embodies provisions relating to expropriation with compensation, the Competition Act, the Companies Act to mention a few all indicate that South Africa's legal regime is not weak or biased against foreigners.[254] The review, however, was concluded on the understanding that FDI had been central to South Africa's economic development but had not been attracted to the country by BITs.[255]

3.3.3 The level of protection afforded to investment

The level of protection afforded to investment was also examined in the review process of South Africa's BITs. In common with many other countries' BITs, South Africa's BITs seek to give foreign investors certain well-established protections and assurances in order to promote foreign investment in the economy including

---

[249]Carrim X 'South Africa and Bilateral Investment Treaties' available at *www.thetradebeat.com%2Fdoc_download%2F17-south-africa-and-bilateral-investment-treaties* (accessed 4 March 2015).

[250] South Africa Info 'Bill provides "robust protection" for investors' available at *http://www.southafrica.info/business/investing/regulations/protection-bill-051113.htm#.VTKVQiFViko* (accessed 4 March 2015).

[251]Williams R 'Nothing Sacred: Developing Countries and the future of International Investment Treaties' available at *http://www.iisd.org/pdf/2011/developing_countries_and_the_future_of_IIAs.pdf* (accessed 3 March 2015).

[252]Williams R 'Nothing Sacred: Developing Countries and the future of International Investment Treaties' available at *http://www.iisd.org/pdf/2011/developing_countries_and_the_future_of_IIAs.pdf* (accessed 3 March 2015).

[253]Williams R 'Nothing Sacred: Developing Countries and the future of International Investment Treaties' available at *http://www.iisd.org/pdf/2011/developing_countries_and_the_future_of_IIAs.pdf* (accessed 3 March 2015).

[254]Carrim X 'South Africa and Bilateral Investment Treaties' available at *www.thetradebeat.com%2Fdoc_download%2F17-south-africa-and-bilateral-investment-treaties* (accessed 4 March 2015).

[255]Carrim X 'Lessons from South Africa`s Bilateral Investment Treaties Review' available at *http://ccsi.columbia.edu/files/2013/10/No_109_-_Carim_-_FINAL.pdf* (accessed 4 March, 2015).

assurances as to expropriation (and compensation where it does occur), security, repatriation of capital and income from investments, equality of treatment with domestic investors and international arbitration of disputes.[256] BITs entered into by South Africa may have extended even greater protection for foreign-owned property against government interference and incursion and without benefit of any meaningful public debate or scrutiny of such a move.[257] Woolfrey expressed the same view by indicating that BITs gave foreign investors greater rights and protection than domestic investors.[258] Such favourable treatment towards foreign investors was indicated earlier in the discussion on the risks that were inherent in South Africa's BITs. To expand on one of the examples that was referred to earlier, South Africa's constitution makes a distinction between deprivation and expropriation while South Africa's BITs do not provide for such a distinction. This indicates greater protection that is provided to foreign investors while local investors were subjected to a narrower definition of the term. This further emphasises that foreign investors were given greater protection than the local investors.

3.4 Measures implemented by South Africa after review

South Africa published its report on the outcome of its review process of the BITs that it had signed together with the measures that it planned to take. This report was meant to draw recommendations or views from the public. After a period of 2 years from the day that the report was published, and based on the findings of this report, the South African government proceeded with its recommendations.[259] The recommendations included five core elements which were the development of a new investment Act, the termination of South Africa's first generation BITs while offering partners the possibility to renegotiate, refraining from entering into BITs in the future unless there were compelling economic and political reasons, to develop a new model BIT as a basis for renegotiation and to establish an Inter-Ministerial

---

[256] Lang J 'Bilateral Investment Treaties- a shield or a sword?' available at *http://www.bowman.co.za/FileBrowser/ArticleDocuments/South-African-Government-Canceling-Bilateral-Investment-Treaties.pdf* (accessed 4 March 2015).

[257] Peterson L 'South Africa's Bilateral Investment Treaties Implications for Development and Human Rights' (2006) 6 *Dialogue on Globalisation Occasional Paper* 22.

[258] Woolfrey S 'Another BIT bites the dust' available at *http://www.tralac.org/discussions/article/5342-another-bit-bites-the-dust.html* (accessed 3 March 2015).

[259] Mossallam M *Process matters: South Africa's experience exiting its BITs* (GEG working paper, University of Oxford 2015/97) 22.

Committee (IMC) to oversee processes.[260] Each of the elements shall be explained further below.

The recommendation to develop a new investment Act has resulted in the drafting of the Promotion and Protection of Investment Bill (PPIB). The PPIB is the outcome of extensive intra-government legal and policy consultations and is certified by South Africa's state law advisors.[261] The PPIB was opened for public comment with various considerations taken from the views expressed by the public.[262] Should Cabinet endorse the PPIB, it would be presented to parliament in 2015 and will eventually enter into force.[263] The PPIB will effectively replace BITs by providing domestic legislation that sets out the rights and obligations of the government and of all investors both local and foreign.[264] On the face of it, the PPIB includes the usual features of BITs while introducing measures that address the concerns identified by the DTIs review.[265] Examples of provisions in the PPIB that address the concerns of the review include, section 6 of the PPIB which imports the concept of national treatment but further qualifies it from South Africa's BITs by reference to applicable legislation in like circumstances.[266] Section 7 of the PPIB provides for equal treatment of both foreign and domestic investors.[267] Section 8 narrows down the definition of expropriation while section 10, is an express provision empowering the

---

[260] Carrim X 'South Africa and Bilateral Investment Treaties' available at *www.thetradebeat.com%2Fdoc_download%2F17-south-africa-and-bilateral-investment-treaties* (accessed 4 March 2015).

[261] De Gama M M 'South Africa`s Promotion and Protection of Investment Bill' available at *www.saiia.org.za%2Fdoc_download%2F688-2015-02-16-fdi-presentation-dr-mustaqeem-de-gama* (accessed 3 March 2015).

[262] De Gama M M 'South Africa`s Promotion and Protection of Investment Bill' available at *www.saiia.org.za%2Fdoc_download%2F688-2015-02-16-fdi-presentation-dr-mustaqeem-de-gama* (accessed 3 March 2015).

[263] De Gama M M 'South Africa`s Promotion and Protection of Investment Bill' available at *www.saiia.org.za%2Fdoc_download%2F688-2015-02-16-fdi-presentation-dr-mustaqeem-de-gama* (accessed 3 March 2015).

[264] Woolfrey S 'South Africa's Promotion and Protection of Investment Bill' available at *http://www.tralac.org/discussions/article/5345-south-africa-s-promotion-and-protection-of-investment-bill.html*(accessed 4 March 2015).

[265] Lang J 'Bilateral Investment Treaties- a shield or a sword?' available at *http://www.bowman.co.za/FileBrowser/ArticleDocuments/South-African-Government-Canceling-Bilateral-Investment-Treaties.pdf* (accessed 4 March 2015).

[266] Lang J 'Bilateral Investment Treaties- a shield or a sword?' available at *http://www.bowman.co.za/FileBrowser/ArticleDocuments/South-African-Government-Canceling-Bilateral-Investment-Treaties.pdf* (accessed 4 March 2015).

[267] Lang J 'Bilateral Investment Treaties- a shield or a sword?' available at *http://www.bowman.co.za/FileBrowser/ArticleDocuments/South-African-Government-Canceling-Bilateral-Investment-Treaties.pdf* (accessed 4 March 2015).

South African government to take measures to redress historical, social and economic inequalities so as to bring the PPIB in line with the objectives of the countries BEE policy.[268] The PPIB provides for a lot more provisions that aim at strengthening the countries investment regime. However, the PPIB omitted the fair and equitable treatment provision and precluded access to international arbitration, which were key concerns highlighted in the outcome of the review.[269] It is important to note that some of these provisions that have been indicated may be changed before the PPIB is enacted.

The review also resulted in the recommendation to terminate first generation BITs. This resulted in South Africa proceeding to legally terminate its expiring BITs with Belgium, Luxembourg, Spain, Germany and Switzerland.[270] These were the first treaties to be terminated by the South African government and were given priority as they were subject to automatic renewal clauses which would have been extended had they not been terminated in time.[271] South Africa further served termination notices to 13 states that it has BITs with, most of which were close to the end of their respective duration and up for renewal.[272] South Africa also indicated that it would address its BIT with China in the context of the BRICS (Brazil, Russia, India, China, South Africa) grouping.[273] Although South Africa has already terminated BITs, served notices to terminate more BITs, protection that was afforded to some of these investments will remain in force for 10-15 years under the so-called survival clause.[274]

---

[268]Ruff D, Kron J, Golsong C 'Bilateral Investment Treaties in South Africa' available at *http://www.nortonrosefulbright.com/knowledge/publications/118456/bilateral-investment-treaties-in-south-africa* (accessed 3 March 2015).

[269]Woolfrey S 'South Africa`s Promotion and Protection of Investment Bill' available at *http://www.tralac.org/discussions/article/5345-south-africa-s-promotion-and-protection-of-investment-bill.html*(accessed 4 March 2015).

[270]UNCTAD 'South Africa Bilateral Investment Treaties' available at *http://investmentpolicyhub.unctad.org/IIA/CountryBits/195#iiaInnerMenu* (accessed 3 March 2015)

[271] Mossallam M *Process matters: South Africa's experience exiting its BITs* (GEG working paper, University of Oxford 2015/97) 13.

[272]Feris J 'Challenging the Status quo- South Africa`s termination of its Bilateral Trade Agreements' available at *https://www.dlapiper.com/en/latinamerica/insights/publications/2014/12/international-arbitration-newsletter-q4-2014/challenging-the-status-quo/* (accessed 3 March 2015).

[273]Kolver L 'SA proceeds with termination of bilateral investment treaties' available at *http://www.wti.org/fileadmin/user_upload/wti.org/00_Press_Downloads/SA_proceeds_with_termination_of_bilateral_investment_treaties.pdf* (accessed 3 March 2015).

[274]Carrim X 'South Africa and Bilateral Investment Treaties' available at *www.thetradebeat.com%2Fdoc_download%2F17-south-africa-and-bilateral-investment-treaties* (accessed 4 March 2015).

Another recommendation from the review was to refrain from entering into BITs in the future unless there were compelling economic and political reasons to do so. The review on the role of BITs in attracting FDI indicated that South Africa does not receive significant inflows of FDI from many partners with whom they had BITs with and yet continued to receive significant investment from jurisdictions with which they have no BITs with.[275] From these and other factors considered during the review, cabinet understood the relationship between BITs and FDI as ambiguous at best and that BITs posed a risk and limitations on the ability of the government to pursue its constitutional-based transformation agenda.[276] As a result, it was concluded that South Africa should refrain from entering into such agreements since the benefits in attracting FDI could not be clearly ascertained.

The fourth recommendation from the review was to develop a new model BIT as a basis for renegotiation. South Africa not only terminated its first generation BITs but also offered partners the possibility to renegotiate.[277] This would be done on the basis of a new model BIT that would aim to reduce the risks inherent in the earlier generation BITs. The new model would also be aligned with national legislation, the constitution and developments in international investment treaty making.[278] As was mentioned earlier, South Africa is both a capital importing and exporting country. A recent Southern African Institute of International Affairs (SAIIA) report notes that South Africa has become one of the top ten investors and trading partner of many African countries.[279] With many South African companies making such extensive investments abroad, BITs would be needed to protect South Africa's investments abroad.[280] Some South African firms have explicitly called for treaties to be put in

---

[275]UNCTAD 'Speaking notes for workshop on Capital Account Regulations and Global Economic Governance UNCTAD/WTO, Geneva 3-4 October' available at *http://unctad.org/meetings/en/Presentation/UNCTAD-GEGI-Carim-2013.pdf* (accessed 3 March 2015).

[276]Lang J 'Bilateral Investment Treaties- a shield or a sword?' available at *http://www.bowman.co.za/FileBrowser/ArticleDocuments/South-African-Government-Canceling-Bilateral-Investment-Treaties.pdf* (accessed 4 March 2015).

[277]Carrim X 'South Africa and Bilateral Investment Treaties' available at *www.thetradebeat.com%2Fdoc_download%2F17-south-africa-and-bilateral-investment-treaties* (accessed 4 March 2015).

[278] Carrim X 'South Africa and Bilateral Investment Treaties' available at *www.thetradebeat.com%2Fdoc_download%2F17-south-africa-and-bilateral-investment-treaties* (accessed 4 March 2015).

[279]Peterson L 'South Africa's Bilateral Investment Treaties Implications for Development and Human Rights' (2006)6 *Dialogue on Globalisation Occasional Paper* 8.

[280]Peterson L 'South Africa's Bilateral Investment Treaties Implications for Development and Human Rights' (2006)6 *Dialogue on Globalisation Occasional Paper* 8.

place before they consider new investments in countries such as Zimbabwe.[281] This indicates why South Africa would still need to maintain a model BIT despite the fact that it is terminating its other agreements. The new model BIT would not only serve to renegotiate old BITs but also in concluding other BITs where necessary.

The fifth recommendation from the review was to establish an Inter-Ministerial Committee (IMC) to oversee the implementation of the aforementioned measures. The committee would be composed of members of various departments namely DTI, the national treasury, the department of international relations and cooperation, the economic development partnership to mention a few that have varying interest in certain provisions of investment agreements.[282] Among other responsibilities, the committee would guide against binding international investment agreements being made by a single department. The IMC has already played a crucial role in the drafting of the PPIB.

3.5 Conclusion

The review process of South Africa's first generation BITs was conducted with the objective of not only uncovering the legal interpretations of BIT provisions or how the BITs co-existed with South Africa's domestic legislation but also on the importance of BITs in attracting FDI in South Africa, the benefits of BITs and the level of protection that was afforded to investment. Being a respondent to an ICSID case prompted South Africa to initiate the review process among other factors. The analyses of the BITs that ensued in both the legal interpretation and in the context of South Africa's domestic legislative framework indicated the problem areas of South Africa's BITs. The role of FDI and the high level of protection afforded to foreign investors that was not proportional to that offered to local investors all contributed to the recommendations on how best the South African government could address the problems that it had regarding its BITs. Based on this review, South Africa made numerous recommendations regarding its outdated BITs which involved the development of a new investment Act, the termination of South Africa's first generation BITs, the suggestion to refrain from entering into more BITs unless there

[281]Peterson L 'South Africa's Bilateral Investment Treaties Implications for Development and Human Rights' (2006)6 *Dialogue on Globalisation Occasional Paper* 8.

[282]Carrim X 'South Africa and Bilateral Investment Treaties' available at *www.thetradebeat.com%2Fdoc_download%2F17-south-africa-and-bilateral-investment-treaties* (accessed 4 March 2015).

were compelling economic and political reasons to do so, the development of a new model BIT as a basis for renegotiation and the establishment of the IMC to oversee processes.

The following chapter will be a comparison of the situation that exists in Kenya now which has a bearing on its outdated BITs to the situation that existed in South Africa prior to review. The chapter will also indicate the lessons that could be learnt from the South African experience that could be applied to the Kenyan context.

Chapter 4: Comparison between the Kenyan and South African BIT experience

4.0 Introduction

This chapter will compare the current situation as it exists in Kenya, which has a bearing on its outdated BITs to the situation that existed in South Africa prior to review. The aim would be to identify the factors that could also prompt Kenya to initiate a review process of its BITs. In addition to this, the chapter will also highlight the lessons that Kenya could learn from South Africa's experience.

4.1 Comparison between Kenya's situation with BITs to South Africa's BIT experience

To provide a better understanding of Kenya's current situation with BITs, it is important to provide a brief history of Kenya in this regard. In the 1970s, Kenya was a prime choice for foreign investors seeking to establish a presence in East Africa.[283] It was during this period that Kenya signed its first BIT with the Netherlands (1970). However, during the 1980s, Kenya's combination of politically driven economic policies, rampant corruption, government malfeasance, sub-standard public services and poor infrastructure discouraged FDI.[284] This spanned over a period of three decades with Kenya being a comparative under performer in attracting FDI.[285] The BITs that Kenya signed with the UK, Italy and Germany were signed during this period that Kenya was receiving low FDI.

In 2002, the newly elected government administration (the 2002-2013 government administration) was handed the reins of a country in crisis following a long period of poor economic and industrial policies and where rampant corruption contributed to a weak investment climate.[286] This new administration was confronted with the need to drastically improve policies and provide a favourable setting for private investment to generate wealth and reduce poverty.[287] Based on this situation, the Kenyan government made the attraction of FDI a priority.[288] Among the measures that the government sought to implement in order to attract FDI was to award many

[283] Kinyanjui S 'The Impact of Terrorism on Foreign Direct Investment in Kenya' (2014) 5 *IJBA*148.
[284] Kinyanjui S 'The Impact of Terrorism on Foreign Direct Investment in Kenya' (2014) 5 *IJBA*148.
[285] UNCTAD *An Investment Guide to Kenya Opportunities and Conditions* (2012) 1.
[286] UNCTAD *Investment Policy Review Kenya*(2005) 3.
[287] UNCTAD *Investment Policy Review Kenya*(2005) 3.
[288] UNCTAD *An Investment Guide to Kenya Opportunities and Conditions* (2012) 13.

incentives such as the tax incentives indicated in chapter 2 among other reforms that were aimed at attracting foreign investors into the country.[289]

However, despite the efforts that the Kenyan Government has made in trying to attract FDI, the amount of FDI that the country has received has not played an important role in the Kenyan economy.[290] Policy makers in Kenya have attributed this low level of FDI to low investor confidence resulting from security and corruption among other factors.[291] As was noted in section 2.2, Kenya has security concerns that arise from terrorist attacks that come from Kenya's neighbouring Somalia. Research has indicated that these terrorist activities have negatively affected the FDI levels in Kenya.[292] Other security concerns can be attributed to the 2007 political violence that erupted in Kenya that dissuaded both tourists and potential investors from coming to Kenya.[293] In addition to this, corruption in Kenya is said to be pervasive and entrenched, and it is also considered one of the major impediments to doing business in Kenya.[294]

From this brief history, it is evident that Kenya's current situation in some way resembles South Africa's situation before the review. What is evident thus far is that both countries entered into their BITs during a period in which the countries needed to attract FDI for economic recovery. What is also evident is that both governments came into power at a time when each respective country needed major economic reforms and other policies to address the social issues that were prevalent at the time. To this end, the new administration in Kenya enacted a new constitution in 2010.[295] Kenya's constitution compares to South Africa's experience with its 1996 constitution in that; both constitutions required the implementation of various reforms that are of a similar nature. For example, as discussed in chapter 3, the South

---

[289] Mwega F M & Ngugi R W 'Foreign Direct Investment in Kenya' in Ajayi S I (ed) *Foreign Direct Investment in Sub-Saharan Africa: Origins, Targets, Impact and Potential* (2006) 124.
[290] Mwega F M & Ngugi R W 'Foreign Direct Investment in Kenya' in Ajayi S I (ed) *Foreign Direct Investment in Sub-Saharan Africa: Origins, Targets, Impact and Potential* (2006) 131.
[291] Mwega F M & Ngugi R W 'Foreign Direct Investment in Kenya' in Ajayi S I (ed) *Foreign Direct Investment in Sub-Saharan Africa: Origins, Targets, Impact and Potential* (2006) 121.
[292] Kinyanjui S 'The Impact of Terrorism on Foreign Direct Investment in Kenya' (2014) 5 *IJBA* 154.
[293] KPMG 'Kenya Country Profile' available at http://www.kpmg.com/Africa/en/KPMG-in-Africa/Documents/Kenya.pdf (accessed 20 March 2015).
[294] U.S Department of State 'Investment Climate Statement 2014' available at http://www.state.gov/e/eb/rls/othr/ics/2014/index.htm (accessed 20 March 2015).
[295] U.S Department of State 'Investment Climate Statement 2014' available at http://www.state.gov/e/eb/rls/othr/ics/2014/index.htm (accessed 20 March 2015).

African constitution obligated its government to create a more open and equitable society based on human rights. This resulted in the initiation of the BEE programs and the MPRDA. Kenya's constitution likewise required the Kenyan government to conduct various discussions on investment related Bills including the Mining Bill that is set to replace the Mining Act of 1940.[296] Kenya's Mining Bill includes reforms in its mining sector which like the MPRDA of South Africa may not be welcome to foreign investors. Kenya's government has already been warned of the prospect of legal action in the event that the Mining Bill is enacted.[297] The arguments raised against the Mining Bill, and the basis of the legal threats were previously discussed in section 2.3.

South Africa has been a respondent to two BIT claims that have been discussed in the previous chapter. Kenya, on the other hand, has not been a respondent to any BIT claims. However, Kenya has been a respondent to an ICSID claim based on an arbitration clause in a concession agreement. In the *World Duty-Free Company v The Republic of Kenya* case, the investor paid a bribe to the then prime minister of Kenya to obtain the right to build and operate duty-free stores at Kenyan airports.[298] A contract was entered into, and the investor spent approximately US$ 27 million building the stores.[299] The investment was subsequently subject to expropriation by a newly instituted government that prompted the investor to seek legal recourse.[300] The tribunal, in this case, rendered the investment agreement secured through bribery illegal, a ruling that was in favour of the Kenyan government.[301]

---

[296] Ong`onge L 'Why Kenya should not sign any more Bilateral Investment Treaties' available at *http://www.ieakenya.or.ke/blog/why-kenya-should-not-sign-any-more-bilateral-investment-treaties* (accessed 20 March 2015).

[297] King and Spalding Client Alert 'Recent Developments: Kenya- What legal options are available to mining companies' available at *http://www.kslaw.com/imageserver/KSPublic/library/publication/ca082013.pdf*(accessed 20 March 2015).

[298] Utterback M, Carroll M & Rich E 'Bribery and Corruption in Foreign Investment: Investor beware' available at *http://www.chinalawinsight.com/2014/08/articles/dispute-resolution/bribery-and-corruption-in-foreign-innvestments-investor-beware/* (accessed 20 March 2015).

[299] Utterback M, Carroll M & Rich E 'Bribery and Corruption in Foreign Investment: Investor beware' available at *http://www.chinalawinsight.com/2014/08/articles/dispute-resolution/bribery-and-corruption-in-foreign-innvestments-investor-beware/* (accessed 20 March 2015).

[300] Utterback M, Carroll M & Rich E 'Bribery and Corruption in Foreign Investment: Investor beware' available at *http://www.chinalawinsight.com/2014/08/articles/dispute-resolution/bribery-and-corruption-in-foreign-innvestments-investor-beware/* (accessed 20 March 2015).

[301] Utterback M, Carroll M & Rich E 'Bribery and Corruption in Foreign Investment: Investor beware' available at *http://www.chinalawinsight.com/2014/08/articles/dispute-resolution/bribery-and-corruption-in-foreign-innvestments-investor-beware/* (accessed 20 March 2015).

With reference to the case mentioned above, the outcome could have been different for the Kenyan government had the investor been protected by a BIT. Although there is evidence of a BIT claim that was dismissed at the ICSID due to corrupt dealings of the foreign investor (*Metal-Tech Ltd v Republic of Uzbekistan*),[302] the earlier chapters of this thesis have demonstrated that ICSID awards in BIT claims are subject to inconsistencies and as such, the outcome of such a case had there been a BIT in force would have been uncertain. Yankee expresses the same view in his comment on the World Duty Free case in which he states that, an ICSID tribunal in a BIT dispute might look to the BIT language to locate an express or implicit anti-corruption rule.[303] Where there is no express mention of bribery or corruption and the BIT is read to implicitly incorporate the term, the interpretation may be subject to inconsistencies.[304]

In the same way in which South Africa developed its legal, regulatory framework from the time that it signed its first BITs, so too has Kenya developed its legal system. Similar to the South African constitution, Kenya's constitution provides protection from the expropriation of private property with the exception of takings in the public interest.[305] Kenya also has sectoral regimes that cover a broad range of sectors with legislation that has a bearing on investors' interests. An example includes the Land Acquisition Act, which governs compensation and the process of acquiring land.[306] However, unlike South Africa's open jurisdiction to providing investment protection that is consistent with the highest standards, Kenyan courts have been described as emerging, with weak institutional capacity and inadequate transparency.[307]

---

[302] Cowley R & Bridi A 'Investor Corruption Bilateral Investment Treaties and International Arbitration: Bribery at Centre of Failed Investor Claim' available at *http://www.nortonrosefulbright.com/knowledge/publications/111529/investor-corruption-bilateral-investment-treaties-and-international-arbitration-bribery-at-centre-of-failed* (accessed 20 March 2015).

[303] Yackee J W 'Investment Treaties and Investor Corruption: An Emerging Defense for Host States?' (2011-2012) 52 *Va. J. Int'l L.* 735.

[304] Yackee J W 'Investment Treaties and Investor Corruption: An Emerging Defense for Host States?' (2011-2012) 52 *Va. J. Int'l L.* 735.

[305] U.S Department of State 'Investment Climate Statement 2014' available at *http://www.state.gov/e/eb/rls/othr/ics/2014/index.htm* (accessed 20 March 2015).

[306] U.S Department of State 'Investment Climate Statement 2014' available at *http://www.state.gov/e/eb/rls/othr/ics/2014/index.htm* (accessed 20 March 2015).

[307] U.S Department of State 'Investment Climate Statement 2014' available at *http://www.state.gov/e/eb/rls/othr/ics/2014/index.htm* (accessed 25 March 2015).

Apart from these legal developments, like South Africa, Kenya is also developing into a capital exporting country.[308] This is principally in the sectors of tourism, manufacturing, retail, finance and media, making the most of its access to the East African Community (EAC) region.[309] There are also reports that domestic investment pulled ahead of FDI in the previous years and has become a key determinant of Kenya's economic performance and prospects.[310] Kenya has also developed into the largest economy amongst members of the EAC.[311] In spite of these developments, as was noted earlier, FDI in Kenya has contributed little to the Gross Domestic Product (GDP) of the country, that is unlike South Africa. With this in mind it is important to point out that Kenya does not have the same type of resources that South Africa has. For example, Kenya's economy is driven largely by agriculture, manufacturing, tourism and real estate sectors.[312] These sectors are highly subject to commodity market price, supply and demand forces, the countries reputation, stability, safety to mention a few. Whereas on the other hand, South Africa has virtual monopolises and is the continent's biggest economy.[313] This indicates that the push and pull factors for FDI in Kenya and South Africa are not the same.

Similar to South Africa, Kenya has also taken part in investment treaty discussions at various levels giving Kenya international exposure to the realities of BITs. Kenya is taking part in the review of the draft EAC model investment treaty following concerns that it does not provide adequate protection for local investors.[314] Kenya also participated in the Common Market for Eastern and Southern Africa (COMESA) negotiations for the COMESA Common Investment Area (CCIA).[315] Additionally,

---

[308] UNCTAD *An Investment Guide to Kenya Opportunities and Conditions* (2012) 14.
[309] UNCTAD *An Investment Guide to Kenya Opportunities and Conditions* (2012) 3.
[310] KPMG 'Kenya Country Profile' available at *http://www.kpmg.com/Africa/en/KPMG-in-Africa/Documents/Kenya.pdf* (accessed 20 March 2015).
[311] Kimeni M S & Kibe J 'Africa's Powerhouse' available at *http://www.brookings.edu/research/opinions/2013/12/30-kenya-economy-kimenyi* (accessed 20 March 2015).
[312] Gundan F 'Kenya Joins Africa's Top 10 Economies After Rebasing of its Gross Domestic Product (GDP)' available at *http://www.forbes.com/sites/faraigundan/2014/10/01/kenya-joins-africas-top-10-economies-after-rebasing-of-its-gross-domestic-product/* (accessed 25 March 2015).
[313] Gundan F 'Kenya Joins Africa's Top 10 Economies After Rebasing of its Gross Domestic Product (GDP)' available at *http://www.forbes.com/sites/faraigundan/2014/10/01/kenya-joins-africas-top-10-economies-after-rebasing-of-its-gross-domestic-product/* (accessed 25 March 2015).
[314] Khisa I 'Talks on EAC –US Trade, Investment deal face hurdles' available at *http://www.theeastafrican.co.ke/business/-investment-deal-face-hurdles/-/2560/2451498/-/hkjlikz/-/index.html* (accessed 20 March 2015).
[315] Press Release 'East Africa: First Round of Negotiations by Regional Negotiating Forum on the COMESA Common Investment Area' available at *http://allafrica.com/stories/200503231018.html* (accessed 20 March 2015).

Kenya is also observing the global trends regarding BITs and how other countries have responded to issues relating to their BITs, including South Africa.

There are many other factors that could be considered for comparison on matters regarding BITs from South Africa's experience and Kenya's current situation. However, the factors that have been discussed above illustrate how Kenya's current situation can relate to South Africa's experience. Furthermore, these factors highlight the necessity for Kenya to learn from the experience that South Africa faced.

4.2 Lessons that Kenya can learn from South Africa's experience

There are many lessons that Kenya could learn from South Africa's BIT experience. From the brief history of South Africa's BITs discussed in section 3.1, Kenya could learn of the need to perform a thorough analysis of the risks and benefits of BITs before entering into them. This would ensure that the agreements are entered into on well thought out decisions. Kenya could use this same principle in weighing the options available to them before renewing or terminating any of its BITs. This ensures that the country does not bind itself to agreements that may later have adverse effects on its development. Learning from South Africa's experience, it would be necessary for Kenya to include the expertise of lawyers and all relevant government stakeholders in the drafting and the negotiation process of BITs. From South Africa's experience, Kenya could also learn that it needs to develop a BIT negotiating strategy particularly when negotiating with traditional capital exporting countries. As was indicated in section 3.3.1.1, South Africa signed BITs that placed all the obligations on the host state and awarded all the rights to the foreign investors. Devising a negotiating strategy would ensure that the BITs are balanced and that both parties get to benefit from the agreements.

Kenya could also learn from the factors that prompted South Africa's review process. It was indicated earlier that at the time when South Africa entered into its BITs there was a common belief among many countries that BITs would attract FDI. It was on this basis that many countries like South Africa entered into BITs. This, however, was not true as was evident from the results of South Africa's review process, and yet South Africa had acted on the common notion that BITs attracted FDI. It was important for South Africa to conduct an assessment of the claims of BITs attracting FDI based on its own situation. The fact that other countries saw BITs as attracting

FDI in their countries did not mean the same would apply to South Africa, as such, a more cautious approach needed to have been taken. Kenya could also use this lesson in making an independent, unbiased decision regarding its BITs bearing in mind all the criticisms that have been highlighted about them. Kenya will need to assess BITs and their effect in its country to examine whether any of the allegations about BITs are indeed true in Kenya's context.

South Africa perceived BITs to be instruments that attract FDI and hastily entered into BITs in the hope of attracting such FDI. However, South Africa's perspective of BITs in the 21st century has changed since it no longer views those same treaties as sources of attracting FDI given that the country is already receiving FDI from countries that do not have BITs with South Africa. This is further corroborated by evidence from other countries such as Brazil that receive FDI even without ratifying any of the BITs that the country signed. From this, Kenya needs to understand that the perspective and rational that countries have when they sign BITs changes over time. Thus, BITs will need to be revaluated continuously to make sure that the motivating factors for concluding them are still relevant.

In addition to this, Kenya could also learn that with each major development that the country undergoes, it should align its treaty provisions with such changes. For example South Africa enacted a new constitution that may be regarded as a major development in the country. The new constitution includes various provisions that in some way have a bearing on its foreign investment treaties. The constitution provides for the protection of property rights and also states the conditions and value to which compensation for expropriation would be awarded. The constitution also provides for the BEE programs that the country has had to implement. As was discussed in the previous chapter, these constitutional provisions contradict some of the provisions in South Africa's BITs and also result in other policies that were not in line with the country's BIT obligations. Economic developments also serve as another example of major developments that the country will need to align with its treaty obligations. As South Africa developed from being a capital importing country to also being a capital exporting country, it had to re-align its BIT obligations with its new developments. The same treaties that the country would have signed when it was still just a capital importing country would not cater for the new developments the country would have undergone as a capital exporting nation.

Another lesson that Kenya could learn from South Africa's experience is the fact that Kenya should not wait for a dispute to be brought against the country over its BIT obligations by foreign investors. Poulsen points out that, decision makers in many developing countries often ignore experiences in other countries which in turn leads to considerable risk-neglect until hit by their first claim.[316] As was noted in section 3.2, South Africa did not initiate the review process of its BITs until the state was a respondent to the Foresti case. The Swiss case against South Africa was an indication that a failure to observe BIT obligations will result in costly awards against the host state. Such situations would be worsened by the fact that legal action under BITs is extremely costly. Moreover, having a decision in one or more ICSID disputes being made against a host state could cause broader damage if outside investors begin to question the environment within the host state.[317] All this goes to highlight how important it is for the Kenyan government to take the necessary action regarding its BITs before any legal dispute emanates from the treaties.

Kenya could also learn from South Africa's participation at both regional and international levels. From such international and regional exposure, Kenya could learn about other countries' issues with BITs and incorporate this knowledge in its BIT policy framework. According to Malik, a debate is healthier in regional dynamics compared to a bilateral context.[318] Malik attributes her views to new model texts and the COMESA treaty that shows African countries that they are not tied to the old European model and that there are ways for innovation in terms of making the treaties more balanced.[319] As was noted earlier, Kenya is also participating in the EAC negotiations for a model treaty and it is also a member of COMESA negotiations, so therefore, Kenya could enhance its knowledge from the participation at such levels and incorporate that knowledge into its BIT policies.

---

[316] Poulsen L N S 'Bounded Rationality and the Diffusion of Modern Investment Treaties' (2014) 58 *International Studies Quarterly* 2.

[317] Allee T & Peinhardt C 'Delegating Differences: Bilateral Investment Treaties and Bargaining Over Dispute Resolution Provision' (2010) 54 *International Studies Quarterly* 3.

[318] Green AR 'Bilateral investment treaties coming back to bite' available at http://www.thisisafricaonline.com/Business/Legal-Bulletin/Bilateral-investment-treaties-coming-back-to-bite(Accessed 20 March 2015).

[319] Green AR 'Bilateral investment treaties coming back to bite' available at http://www.thisisafricaonline.com/Business/Legal-Bulletin/Bilateral-investment-treaties-coming-back-to-bite(Accessed 20 March 2015).

Kenya could also gain from the measures that South Africa adopted after its review process. The South African PPIB that is set to govern investments both foreign and domestic has faced huge amounts of criticism. The PPIB has been criticised for reducing the amount of compensation to be paid in the event of expropriation from market value to the deemed fair and equitable value.[320] The PPIB has also been criticised for limiting disputes to domestic dispute resolution mechanisms and subjecting foreign investors to the same cumbersome regulatory environment to redress past inequalities as imposed on local investors.[321] Some of the critics of the PPIB include the American Chamber of Commerce (AmCham) that is formed by South Africans in Johannesburg[322] and the South Africa-German Chamber of Commerce and Industry which warned that the termination of the BITs could have a negative impact on investor confidence.[323] The PPIB has also been criticised for its lack of ability to protect South Africa's outbound investments.[324] In addition to this, South Africa will still be subject to its obligations under the Southern Africa Development Community (SADC) Protocol on Trade and Investment (2006) regardless of the fact that the PPIB is enacted or not.[325] This protocol requires member states to create a favourable investment climate in the region by, among other actions, not expropriating investments except for a public purpose against prompt, adequate and effective compensation, and allowing access to international arbitration.[326] Such requirements are not in line with the new PPIB that is set to be promulgated. With this in mind, Kenya could learn of the shortcomings of resorting to

---

[320] Reuters 'South Africa Investment Law Overhaul Sparks Concerns' available at *http://www.safpi.org/news/article/2013/south-africa-investment-law-overhaul-sparks-concerns* (Accessed 20 March 2015).

[321] Reuters 'South Africa Investment Law Overhaul Sparks Concerns' available at *http://www.safpi.org/news/article/2013/south-africa-investment-law-overhaul-sparks-concerns* (Accessed 20 March 2015).

[322] Parly Report SA 'Promotion and Protection of Investment Bill opens up major row' available at *http://parlyreportsa.co.za/finance-economic/promotion-and-protection-of-investment-bill-opens-major-row/* (Accessed 20 March 2015).

[323] Woolfrey S 'Another BIT bites the dust' available at *http://www.tralac.org/discussions/article/5342-another-bit-bites-the-dust.html* (accessed 20 March 2015).

[324] Lang J 'Bilateral Investment Treaties- a shield or a sword?' available at *http://www.bowman.co.za/FileBrowser/ArticleDocuments/South-African-Government-Canceling-Bilateral-Investment-Treaties.pdf* (accessed 20 March 2015).

[325] Feris J 'Challenging the Status Quo- South Africa`s termination of its Bilateral Trade Agreements' available at *https://www.dlapiper.com/en/latinamerica/insights/publications/2014/12/international-arbitration-newsletter-q4-2014/challenging-the-status-quo/* (accessed 20 March 2015).

[326] Feris J 'Challenging the Status Quo- South Africa`s termination of its Bilateral Trade Agreements' available at *https://www.dlapiper.com/en/latinamerica/insights/publications/2014/12/international-arbitration-newsletter-q4-2014/challenging-the-status-quo/* (accessed 20 March 2015).

domesticating BITs and thereby seek to lessen the consequences or avoid the option.

Another lesson that could be learnt from the PPIB that South Africa seeks to utilise is that such a measure could be useful if the legal and judiciary system of the country is of a high standard. As was previously discussed, South Africa's judiciary system is regarded as being equivalent to international standards. As such, South Africa can resort to domesticating its BITs with the expectation that foreign investors would be confident in their judicial system. Strengthening the role of national courts could mean that foreign investors may be required to submit disputes that arise during the course of foreign investment to the investment host state's national courts in the first instance rather than being able to go straight to international tribunals.[327] Encouraging such states to develop their legal regimes in order to cope with the demands of settling international investment disputes will also enable them to free themselves from the sometimes arbitrary rulings in international investment tribunals that often award huge amounts of compensation to foreign investors, which the state has to pay.[328] This requires Kenya to learn the importance of upgrading its system so that it meets international standards and can settle investment disputes in-country rather than having them settled outside their jurisdiction.

Kenya could also learn from the manner in which South Africa terminated its BITs. South Africa has been criticised for the lack of adequate communication and re-assurance to the state parties when it terminated its BITs.[329] The EU ambassador was quoted as stating that the decision to terminate the BITs with EU countries should have been a result of broader consultation.[330] The World Trade Institute International Investment Initiative Director was also quoted as stating that the process through which South Africa decided to terminate its BITs had in fact

[327] Butler N 'The State of International Investment Arbitration: The Possibility of Establishing An Appeal Mechanism' (unpublished Ph.D thesis, The University of Leeds, 2012) 153.
[328] Butler N 'The State of International Investment Arbitration: The Possibility of Establishing An Appeal Mechanism' (unpublished Ph.D thesis, The University of Leeds, 2012) 154.
[329] Reuters 'South Africa Investment Law Overhaul Sparks Concerns' available at *http://www.safpi.org/news/article/2013/south-africa-investment-law-overhaul-sparks-concerns* (Accessed 20 March 2015).
[330] Kolver L 'South Africa proceeds with termination of Bilateral Investment Treaties' available at *http://www.engineeringnews.co.za/article/sa-proceeds-with-termination-of-bilateral-investment-treaties-2013-10-21* (Accessed 20 March 2015).

impacted FDI confidence.[331] This may be because the decision was made unilaterally by South Africa not appearing to have considered the possibility of at least attempting to renegotiate the terms of the terminated BITs.[332] Moreover, the termination was done before the enactment of the PPIB that was meant to replace the protection offered by BITs.[333] Kenya could learn from the criticism South Africa faced so as to avoid the same situation for Kenya. Kenya could also learn from the fact that South Africa did not withdraw from any active treaty in an effort to protect diplomatic relations.[334]

4.3 Conclusion

In conclusion, it can be noted that Kenya's current situation does not differ substantially from the one that existed in South Africa prior to the review of its BITs. Having such a similar situation to a country that has reviewed its BITs, Kenya should learn from the experiences that South Africa underwent. These lessons were drawn from the factors that necessitated the review, the manner in which the review was undertaken and the measures that were taken as a result of South Africa's review process.

The next chapter will recommend possible measures that Kenya's government could implement with respect to the country's outdated BITs. The chapter will recommend actions that the Kenyan government can take in light of their own situation. This will also be the concluding chapter of this thesis.

---

[331]Kolver L 'South Africa proceeds with termination of Bilateral Investment Treaties' available at *http://www.engineeringnews.co.za/article/sa-proceeds-with-termination-of-bilateral-investment-treaties-2013-10-21* (Accessed 20 March 2015).

[332] Woolfrey S 'Another BIT bites the dust' available at *http://www.tralac.org/discussions/article/5342-another-bit-bites-the-dust.html* (accessed 20 March 2015).

[333] Woolfrey S 'Another BIT bites the dust' available at *http://www.tralac.org/discussions/article/5342-another-bit-bites-the-dust.html* (accessed 20 March 2015).

[334] Green A R 'Bilateral investment treaties coming back to bite' available at http://www.thisisafricaonline.com/Business/Legal-Bulletin/Bilateral-investment-treaties-coming-back-to-bite(Accessed 20 March 2015).

Chapter 5: Conclusion and Recommendations

5.0 Introduction

This chapter provides a summary of the main issues of the study and also provides recommendations for Kenya's government with respect to its outdated BITs.

5.1 Summary

The study presented a comparative analysis between Kenya and South Africa regarding BITs signed prior to the 21st century. In particular, the study examined factors such as how these BITs have been considered as restricting policy space of the host state, how these BITs have been unfairly skewed towards foreign investors and how BITs, in general, have resulted in a large number of cases at ICISD.

The analysis of Kenya's BITs revealed that some of the BITs omitted to define important terms and where the terms were defined in the other treaties; the definitions could be subject to very broad interpretations. The analysis also revealed that there is not enough detail on what the fair and equitable treatment provision entails or enough detail to limit the scope of application of the most favoured nation provision that may result in undesirable interpretations for the Kenyan government. Various cases were presented that show how the BIT provisions that were highlighted could affect Kenya, and these cases pointed out the uncertainties that plague the dispute settlement forums that are mainly used in investment disputes. Kenya's BITs place a limit on the Kenyan government's policy space in matters regarding the assistance of its own nationals due to the national treatment provision and on promulgating new legislation that affects investors' investments.

Furthermore, the study also revealed that South Africa entered into its BITs without a proper appreciation of what the South African government was signing up for. The desire of South Africa's government to attract FDI and eliminate all forms of racial inequalities resulted in South Africa being sued at international tribunals, prompting the initiation of the review of South Africa's BITs. The review process of South Africa's first generation BITs was targeted to specific areas with the participation of various stakeholders. The review revealed that the BIT provisions were not what South Africa desired to be bound to, as some of the provisions were a direct violation of South Africa's constitution and South African legislation. With this in mind, South

Africa made numerous recommendations regarding its outdated BITs which involved the development of a new investment Act, the termination of South Africa's first generation BITs, the suggestion to refrain from entering into more BITs unless there were compelling economic and political reasons to do so, to develop a new model BIT as a basis for renegotiation and to establish the IMC to oversee processes.

The comparison of Kenya's current situation to the one that existed in South Africa before the review is substantially the same. Having such a similar situation to a country that has reviewed its BITs, Kenya has numerous lessons to learn from South Africa.These lessons were drawn from the factors that necessitated the review, the manner in which the review was undertaken and the measures that were taken as a result of South Africa's review process. The following section describes specific recommendations for Kenya in light of South Africa's experiences with dealing with BITs signed prior to the 21st century.

5.2 Recommendations

5.2.1 Review BITs

The first recommendation for Kenya is that it should carry out an extensive BIT review process that is targeted at uncovering specific aspects. Kenya's BIT review could be aimed at ascertaining if BITs still fall in line with Kenya's domestic legislative agenda and the country's goals of attracting FDI. Kenya could also assess the vulnerabilities in the language of its current BITs that would open up Kenya to litigation. In addition, Kenya could also determine if BITs will attract enough FDI to balance the risks of claims that could be brought upon Kenya. Whilst Kenya is similar to South Africa in that they are both African countries seeking to increase their FDI and bolster their economies, each country has its own unique aspects indicated in the previous chapter. With this in mind, even though Kenya can take lessons from South Africa, carrying out their own BIT review will help them understand whether BITs work for their specific situation that is the combination of their characteristics which make Kenya a unique country. Based on the results of the review, Kenya could terminate BITs currently enforced, maintain a BIT system or find alternative measures of protecting and promoting FDI. Each of these measures shall be further discussed below.

5.2.2 Terminate current BITs

Kenya should consider terminating its current BITs. All of Kenya's BITs that have been discussed in this thesis allow for the termination of the agreements upon written notice within the prescribed time frame indicated in the BITs. Kenya could therefore serve notices of termination to its BIT contracting partners. In this regard, Kenya should take into consideration the diplomatic downsides of unilaterally terminating BITs without offering the contracting partners the possibility of renegotiating the agreements.[335] With this in mind it would be important for Kenya to assess the benefits of maintaining the BIT system. Alternatively, Kenya could terminate the agreements upon a mutual agreement by the negotiating partners. This would ensure that Kenya resorts to a measure that is beneficial for the Kenyan government.

5.2.3 Maintaining a BIT system

5.2.3.1 Benefits of maintaining the BIT system

As was mentioned above, Kenya should also assess the benefits of maintaining a BIT system that is specific for Kenya and may be used as a basis for renegotiating its old BITs. Some of the factors that Kenya could consider in assessing BIT importance for Kenya include the fact that some investors do consider BITs before investing in a country as is evident from issues such as treaty shopping for instance, where investors choose to invest in countries that have a BIT with the host country rather than investing in their home country.[336] Historical experience as well as recent developments in parts of Latin America has also shown that resource extraction sectors are particularly prone to discrimination or even predatory government interference.[337] As such, natural resource investors may take more notice of BITs. This is important for Kenya to consider since the country has recent discoveries of oil

[335] Woolfrey S 'Another BIT bites the dust' available at *http://www.tralac.org/discussions/article/5342-another-bit-bites-the-dust.html* (accessed 20 March 2015).

[336] Poulsen L N S 'The Importance of BITs for Foreign Direct Investment and Political Risk Insurance: Revisiting the Evidence' in Sauvant K P (ed) *Yearbook on International Investment Law and Policy* (2010) 3.

[337] Poulsen L N S 'The Importance of BITs for Foreign Direct Investment and Political Risk Insurance: Revisiting the Evidence' in Sauvant K P (ed) *Yearbook on International Investment Law and Policy* (2010) 8.

and gas that are expected to attract the interest of many foreign investors who may consider having BITs with Kenya in order to protect their investments.[338]

In addition to the aforementioned factors, Ginsburg indicates that it would be part of due diligence for an investor to look for the existence of a BIT before investing.[339] If investors exercise such due diligence, there would be interests in the Kenyan BIT system from investors seeking to invest in Kenya. Moreover, empirical research has also shown that states with high political risk stand to gain the most inbound investment by concluding investment treaties.[340] As was discussed previously, Kenya is perceived as having risk not only from terrorist attacks but also from a dented reputation from the 2007 political violence. Another important consideration for maintaining a BIT system for Kenya would be for the protection of Kenya's investments abroad. The protection that these BITs offer to investors has been evident in the increase in the number of cases in the last decades that may make investors more diligent about protecting their investments. All these advantages listed suggest a strong need for Kenya to maintain a BIT system. The negative consequences of BITs from other countries' experiences in the past do not mean that such effects cannot be avoided. Additionally, it is important to note that the result of an analysis of the risks and benefits of BITs in one country is not going to necessarily be the same as in the other. The BIT system would, however, need to be tailored in a manner that is favourable to Kenya's current situation as discussed further below.

5.2.3.2 Manner in which BIT system should be drafted

The recommended BIT system for Kenya should consist of a new model BIT that is formulated in a manner that caters for the shortfalls of Kenya's earlier BITs while also reflecting the country's developmental needs. Kenya should include the definitions of the terms 'investment' and 'investor' in the new model and ensure that these definitions are included in all subsequent agreements. Additionally, Kenya should ensure that with the terms are defined in a manner that takes into

---

[338] Stafford J 'All Eyes On Kenya: The Next Big Oil Exporter' available at http://oilprice.com/Energy/Crude-Oil/All-Eyes-on-Kenya-The-Next-Big-Oil-Exporter.html (accessed 20 March 2015).

[339] Ginsburg R 'Political Risk Insurance and Bilateral Investment Treaties: Making the Connection' (2013) 14 *The Journal of World Investment and Trade* 944.

[340] Brower C N & Blanchard S 'From "Dealing in Virtue" to "Profiting from Injustice": The Case Against "Re-Statification" of Investment Dispute Settlement' (2014) 55 *Harvard International Law Journal* 59.

consideration the disadvantages of the current BIT definitions that were discussed in section 2.2. For example, Kenya could expound on the criteria used in determining nationality rather than merely stating that it should be in accordance with national laws. Kenya could also express what the FIPA defines as investments in the Kenyan BIT model. Kenya may also elaborate further on what the fair and equitable treatment entails. With regards to the protection and security clause, the COMESA BIT model, among other newer texts, is said to have totally excluded the provision from the BITs.[341] However, for the Kenyan government, despite its huge burden and the risks involved in the event that attacks are made on foreign investment property, Kenya could maintain the provision in its BITs as a way of signalling its true commitment to protecting foreign investor's property. The provision may be included with a limitation of liability for the Kenyan government. Kenya would, therefore, need to intensify its efforts in ensuring that it curbs terrorism so as to avoid guaranteeing what it cannot provide which may result in legal action. Such efforts would attract investments of those foreigners that have hesitated to invest in Kenya based on security concerns. The national treatment provision may be phrased to ensure that the Kenyan government may be able to assist its local industries in like circumstances to grow while the MFN provision may be phrased in a manner that indicates the extent to which the provision should apply.

The investor-state dispute provision being included or excluded from BITs is one that has raised different views. As was explained in earlier chapters, the investor-state dispute provision is a one-way process of public law claims where only one class of parties (the investor) triggers use of the system by bringing claims and only the other class (host states) is liable to pay awards for violating the treaty.[342] In South Africa, a group tasked with reviewing South Africa's policy recommended that South Africa omit dispute mechanisms to which investors have had direct access.[343] This recommendation was based on the fact that South African laws provide protection of

[341]Green AR 'Bilateral investment treaties coming back to bite' available at http://www.thisisafricaonline.com/Business/Legal-Bulletin/Bilateral-investment-treaties-coming-back-to-bite(Accessed 20 March 2015).

[342]Harten G V 'Five Justifications For Investment Treaties: A Critical Discussion' (2010) 2 *Trade L. & Dev. 19* 37.

[343]Klaaren J & Schneiderman D *Investor-State Arbitration and South Africa's Bilateral Investment Treaty Policy Framework Review* (comment submitted to the DTI, Mandela Institute 2009) 2.

investments, including how those investments are handled in the country.[344] It has been reported that the EU is engaged in a heated debate over the value of investor-state dispute provisions as it negotiates with the US over a trade and investment deal.[345] Germany has joined France in stating that it would oppose this mechanism in the transatlantic deal.[346] Many other countries have opposed the inclusion of this provision in their BITs. However, Malaysia affirmed benefits of investor-state arbitration to developing countries by publishing a report in which it confirmed its continued commitment to investor-state arbitration to promote its economic developments.[347] The Malaysian report was an official response to critics of the mechanism and this report further advised states that have for various reasons, decided to opt out and would-be reformers should refrain from tinkering with the system and undermining its stability to fulfil its intended purpose for those that wish to use it.[348] Malaysia has not alone in affirming the relevant of the investor-state dispute provision in its BITs as there is evidence on the UNCTAD Investment Policy Hub of new BITs and IIAs that are still being concluded with the investor-state dispute provision.[349] Considering these varying views on the provision, the recommendation for Kenya is that they should consider maintaining the investor-state dispute provision in its model BIT for reasons discussed below.

Allee and Peinhardt express the view that, home governments will see less need to rely on ICSID when the host country possesses greater respect for the rule of law.[350] As was discussed previously, Kenya's judicial system is one that is still emerging with a new constitution that has brought about reforms that are still to be implemented. The effects of such reforms are yet to be evaluated by prospective

---

[344]Klaaren J & Schneiderman D *Investor-State Arbitration and South Africa's Bilateral Investment Treaty Policy Framework Review* (comment submitted to the DTI, Mandela Institute 2009) 2.

[345] Bland B & Donnan S 'Indonesia to terminate more than 60 Bilateral Investment Treaties' available at *http://www.ft.com/intl/cms/s/0/3755c1b2-b4e2-11e3-af92-00144feabdc0.html#axzz3XyZ2mmel* (accessed 20 March 2015).

[346] Bland B & Donnan S 'Indonesia to terminate more than 60 Bilateral Investment Treaties' available at *http://www.ft.com/intl/cms/s/0/3755c1b2-b4e2-11e3-af92-00144feabdc0.html#axzz3XyZ2mmel* (accessed 20 March 2015).

[347]Brower C N & Blanchard S 'From "Dealing in Virtue" to "Profiting from Injustice": The Case Against "Re-Statification" of Investment Dispute Settlement' (2014) 55 *Harvard International Law Journal* 59.

[348]Brower C N & Blanchard S 'From "Dealing in Virtue" to "Profiting from Injustice": The Case Against "Re-Statification" of Investment Dispute Settlement' (2014) 55 *Harvard International Law Journal* 59.

[349] UNCTAD 'Investment Policy Review' available at *http://investmentpolicyhub.unctad.org/IIA/iiasByCountry#iiaInnerMenu* (accessed 25 March 2015).

[350] Allee T & Peinhardt C 'Delegating Differences: Bilateral Investment Treaties and Bargaining Over Dispute Resolution Provision' (2010) 54 *International Studies Quarterly* 10.

foreign investors. In addition to this, in Kenya, investors have a poor opinion of the court system.[351] The World Bank's World Business Environment Survey (WBES) indicates that 74 percent of investors rated the overall quality of the court system as 'slightly bad', 'bad' or 'very bad' as opposed to 'slightly good', 'good' or 'very good'.[352] There have also been several incidents in which high court and appeal court judges were suspended for alleged corruption.[353] With such situations and perceptions of Kenya's judicial system, maintaining the investor-state dispute provision would provide confidence to foreign investors knowing that they will have access to an independent and fair ruling in the event of a dispute. It is also important to note that the investor-state arbitration also has its disadvantages to the investor that may also deter the investor from resorting to the mechanism unless it is necessary. The mechanism entails significant costs for the investor, costs that may not be recouped from any eventual arbitral award and it also serves to rupture those relationships between the investor and the state which could even put in question the investor's relationships with other countries that are sympathetic to the host country respondent.[354] With this in mind, Kenya could maintain the investor-state arbitration provision in its BIT model.

With regards to the manner in which the provision should be phrased in Kenya's BITs, the new model BIT should avoid pre-consent to investor initiated arbitration which is evident in Article 8 (1) of the UK BIT that has been discussed in chapter 2. Pre-consent to investor initiated enforceable arbitration for a wide range of investment disputes may seriously constrain the host states policy autonomy.[355] It is for this reason that a number of states have sought to limit their exposure to adverse awards and to preserve a greater degree of policy autonomy vis-à-vis foreign investors by offering carefully tailored promises to consent to arbitration rather than

---

[351] UNCTAD *Investment Policy Review Kenya*(2005) 40.

[352] UNCTAD *Investment Policy Review Kenya*(2005) 40.

[353] UNCTAD *Investment Policy Review Kenya*(2005) 40.

[354] Salacuse J W 'Is There a Better Way? Alternative Methods to Treaty-Based, Investor-State Dispute Resolution' (2007) 31 *Fordham International Law Journal* 147.

[355] Yackee J W 'Conceptual Difficulties in the Empirical Study of Bilateral Investment Treaties' (2007-2008) 33 *Brook. J. Int'l L. 405*426.

actual pre-consent.[356] Kenya could also consider making the dispute settlement provision only relevant to certain clauses of the BIT.

With the suggestion of a new BIT model in mind, Kenya could seek to renegotiate its old BITs and enter into new BITs only where necessary for the Kenyan government to do so. In drafting this new model BIT, Kenya should include the participation of all stakeholders that may directly or indirectly be affected by any of the provisions in the BIT model and the participation of the public. It will also be important for Kenya to consider raising awareness of their BITs to Kenyan citizens. The drafters of this new model should anticipate how the treaty provisions will be understood by outside users and, above all, by arbitration panels.[357] The draft model should be construed with wording that carries legal effects in a manner that caters for Kenyan investments abroad while also including other development needs that the Kenyan government may wish to achieve. All this should be aimed at achieving a balance between the investor's rights and the host states obligations. The Kenyan government should also ensure that there is a central body that governs issues that relate to BITs; a suggestion that was akin to the IMC that was established in South Africa to manage the negotiation of BITs. This shift in BIT treaty formation will thereby require Kenya to better articulate its individual needs in BITs and help the country negotiate the agreements from a position of strength.[358]

5.2.4 Capacity-building

The recommendation for Kenya to adopt an effective new model BIT necessarily requires that Kenya, consider capacity-building for all the officials that would be involved in handling BITs. By building capacity and increasing awareness of the consequences of concluding investment treaties, African states will, carefully examine the meaning and consider the provisions before signing such treaties.[359]

---

[356] Yackee J W 'Conceptual Difficulties in the Empirical Study of Bilateral Investment Treaties' (2007-2008) 33 *Brook. J. Int'l L. 405*426.

[357] Gordon K &Pohl J 'Investment Treaties Over Time-Treaty Practice and Interpretation in a Changing World' 2015/02 *OECD*24.

[358]Masamba M 'Africa and bilateral investment treaties: to "BIT" or not?' available at *http://www.consultancyafrica.com/index.php?option=com_content&view=article&id=1697:africa-and-bilateral-investment-treaties-to-bit-or-not&catid=82:african-industry-a-business&Itemid=266*(Accessed 19 October 2014).

[359]Green AR 'Bilateral investment treaties coming back to bite' available at http://www.thisisafricaonline.com/Business/Legal-Bulletin/Bilateral-investment-treaties-coming-back-to-bite(Accessed 20 March 2015).

This would go a long way in avoiding disputes involving African states.[360] The African International Legal Awareness (AILA) was founded in 2011 and has organised BIT training workshops for government lawyers with some of the training being held within countries that would have requested such training.[361] The Trade Law Centre for Southern Africa (Tralac) has also organised BIT training workshops for government officials such as the workshop that was held in Zimbabwe on BIT negotiation training in August 2014.[362] The International Institute for Sustainable Development (IISD) has also conducted training courses for African government officials' in-country and at a regional level.[363] Kenya should also ensure that its government officials are well trained and informed on matters regarding BITs.

5.2.5 Alternative measures

In the event that BITs are determined to be ineffective, Kenya could come up with creative solutions that are not BIT-model dependent. For example, the Kenyan government could also consider the possibility of resorting to investment contracts. Investment contracts can be regarded as a form of legal instrument that could help alleviate investor concerns about political risks and yet still allow host states to moderate their commitments on a case by case basis.[364] Investment contracts are also beneficial in that they provide the investor with the opportunity to spell out his rights and obligations vis-à-vis the state with far greater precision and completeness than the rights and obligations contained in the typical BIT which represents a one-size-fits-all solution that is unlikely to ideally suit all investors.[365] Such contracts could also bear the same standards as the BITs including recourse to international

[360]Green AR 'Bilateral investment treaties coming back to bite' available at http://www.thisisafricaonline.com/Business/Legal-Bulletin/Bilateral-investment-treaties-coming-back-to-bite(Accessed 20 March 2015).

[361] Baruti R 'Building International Investment Law Expertise For Africa' available at *http://www.innovatingjustice.com/innovations/building-international-investment-law-expertise-for-africa* (Accessed 20 March 2015).

[362]Trade Law Centre 'Training Programme-Drafting and Negotiating Investment Treaties: Zimbabwe, August 2014' available at *http://www.tralac.org/events/article/6085-training-programme-drafting-and-negotiating-investment-treaties-zimbabwe-august-2014* (accessed 20 March 2015).

[363] Green A R 'Bilateral investment treaties coming back to bite' available at http://www.thisisafricaonline.com/Business/Legal-Bulletin/Bilateral-investment-treaties-coming-back-to-bite(Accessed 20 March 2015).

[364] Poulsen L N S 'Bounded Rationality and the Diffusion of Modern Investment Treaties' (2014) 58 *International Studies Quarterly* 1.

[365] Yackee J W 'Conceptual Difficulties in the Empirical Study of Bilateral Investment Treaties' (2007-2008) 33 *Brook. J. Int'l L. 405*452.

arbitration backed by the New York or ICSID Conventions.[366] With such an alternative, the Kenyan government could still provide investors with the protection they desire given that BITs are mainly sought for the protection they provide to foreign investments. Kenya's outward investors could also seek to negotiate such contracts stating the terms upon which the investment is to be governed in the host country.

5.2.6 Other recommendations

In addition to either maintaining a BIT system or signing investment contracts, Kenya could also work on developing its judiciary system so that it meets international standards. By so doing, Kenya could thereafter work at governing its investment, relying more on its domestic legislation rather than international instruments that have negative consequences that were highlighted in the earlier chapters. Strengthening the role of national courts could mean that foreign investors may be required to submit disputes that arise during the course of foreign investment to the investment host states national courts, rather than being able to go straight to international tribunals.[367] BITs could then in future be re-negotiated to provide for domestic dispute resolution.

5.3 Final Remarks

Kenya should review its BITs targeted at ascertaining if BITs still fall in line with Kenya's legislation, ascertaining the vulnerabilities in the language of current BITs and ascertaining if BITs will attract enough FDI to balance the risks of claims that could be brought upon Kenya. Based on the outcome of the review, Kenya should consider terminating its BITs that are currently enforced, maintain a BIT system to be used were necessary, work on building capacity and consider the possibilities of alternative measures that are not BIT-model dependant.

[366] Poulsen L N S 'Bounded Rationality and the Diffusion of Modern Investment Treaties' (2014) 58 *International Studies Quarterly* 1.
[367] Butler N 'The State of International Investment Arbitration: The Possibility of Establishing An Appeal Mechanism' (unpublished Ph.D thesis, The University of Leeds, 2012) 153.

Bibliography

Books

Cheng, Everaert, Jonas et al *Kenya, Uganda and United Republic of Tanzania: Selected Issues* (2008) Washington DC: International Monetary Fund.

Sornarajah M *The International Law on Foreign Investment* (2012) Cambridge: Cambridge University Press

UNCTAD *An Investment Guide to Kenya Opportunities and Conditions* (2012) United Nations.

UNCTAD *Investment Policy Review Kenya* (2005) United Nations.

Chapters in Books

Mwega F M & Ngugi R W 'Foreign Direct Investment in Kenya' in Ajayi S I (ed) *Foreign Direct Investment in Sub-Saharan Africa: Origins, Targets, Impact and Potential* (2006) African Economic Research Consortium.

Poulsen L N S 'The Importance of BITs for Foreign Direct Investment and Political Risk Insurance: Revisiting the Evidence' in Sauvant K P (ed) *Yearbook on International Investment Law and Policy* (2010) New York: Oxford University Press.

Journals

Allee T & Peinhardt C 'Delegating Differences: Bilateral Investment Treaties and Bargaining Over Dispute Resolution Provision' (2010) 54 *International Studies Quarterly* 1-26.

Bernasconi-Osterwalder N & Johnson L 'Belgium's Model Bilateral Investment Treaty: A Review' 2010 *International Institute For Sustainable Development (IISD)* 1-28.

Bernasconi-Osterwalder N & Johnson L 'Commentary to the Austrian Model Investment Treaty' 2011 *IISD* 1-42.

Brower C N & Blanchard S 'From "Dealing in Virtue" to "Profiting from Injustice": The Case Against "Re-Statification" of Investment Dispute Settlement' (2014) 55 *Harvard International Law Journal* 45-59.

Cole T 'The Boundaries of Most Favored Nation Treatment in International Investment Law' (2012) 33 *Michigan Journal of International Law* 537-586.

Dolzer R 'The Impact of International Investment Treaties on Domestic Administrative Law' (2006) 37 *International Law and Politics* 953-972.

Figanmese I A 'The Impact of the Maffezini Decision on the Interpretation of MFN Clauses in Investment Treaties' (2011) 8 *Ankara Law Review* 221-237.

Ginsburg T 'International Substitutes for Domestic Institutions: Bilateral Investment Treaties and Governance' (2005) 25 *International Review of Law and Economics* 107-123.

Ginsburg R 'Political Risk Insurance and Bilateral Investment Treaties: Making the Connection' (2013) 14 *The Journal of World Investment and Trade* 943-977.

Ghouri A A 'The Evolution of bilateral investment treaties, investment treaty arbitration and international investment law' (2011) 14 (6) *Int. A.L.R* 196.

Gordon K &Pohl J 'Investment Treaties Over Time- Treaty Practice and Interpretation in a Changing World' 2015/02 *OECD* 1-42.

Harten G V 'Five Justifications For Investment Treaties: A Critical Discussion' (2010) 2 *Trade L. & Dev.* 19-58.

Johnson A R 'Rethinking Bilateral Investment Treaties for Sub-Saharan Africa' (2009-2010) 59 *Emory L. J.* 919-968.

Kinyanjui S 'The Impact of Terrorism on Foreign Direct Investment in Kenya' (2014) 5 *IJBA* 148-157.

Mann H 'International Investment Agreements, Business and Human Rights: Key Issues and Opportunities' 2008 *IISD* 1-43.

Malik M 'Time for a Change. Germanys Bilateral Investment Treaty Programme and Development Policy' (2006) 27 *Dialogue on Globalisation Occassional Paper* 1-48.

Malik M 'Recent Developments in the Definitions of Investment in International Investment Agreements' 2008 *IISD* 1-24.

Mosoti V 'Bilateral Investment Treaties and the possibility of a multilateral framework on investment at the WTO: are poor economies caught in between' (2005) 26 *Nw. J. Int'l L. & Bus.* 95-138.

Parker S L 'A BIT at a Time: The Proper Extension of the MFN Clause to Dispute Settlement Provisions in Bilateral Investment Treaties' (2012) 2 *Arbitration Brief* 30-63.

Peterson L 'Bilateral Investment Treaties and Development Policy-Making' 2004 *IISD 1*-27.

Peterson L 'South Africa's Bilateral Investment Treaties Implications for Development and Human Rights' (2006) 6 *Dialogue on Globalisation Occasional Paper* 1-44.

Peterson L E & Garland R 'Bilateral Investment Treaties and Land Reform in Southern Africa' 2010 *Rights and Democracy International Centre for Human Rights and Democratic Development* 1-17.

Poulsen L N S 'Bounded Rationality and the Diffusion of Modern Investment Treaties' (2014) 58 *International Studies Quarterly* 1-14.

Ranjan P 'India and Bilateral Investment Treaties- A Changing Landscape' (2014) 29 *ICSID Review* 419-450

Salacuse J W 'Is There a Better Way? Alternative Methods to Treaty-Based, Investor-State Dispute Resolution' (2007) 31 *Fordham International Law Journal* 138-185.

Schreuer C 'Fair and Equitable Treatment in Arbitral Practice' (2005) 6 *The Journal of World Investment and Trade* 356-386.

Sheffer M W 'Bilateral Investment Treaties a Friend or Foe of Human Rights?' (2010-2011) 39:3 *Den. J. Int'l L. & Pol'y* 483-521.

Ukpe A 'Applicability of the Most-Favoured-Nation Clause to Dispute Settlement Provisions in Bilateral Investment Treaties: A Uniform Approach?' (2011-2012) 11 *Centre For Energy, Petroleum and Mineral Law Policy Annual Review(CEPMLP Annual Review)* 1-21.

Yackee J W 'Conceptual Difficulties in the Empirical Study of Bilateral Investment Treaties' (2007-2008) 33 *Brook. J. Int'l L.* 405-462.

Yackee J W 'Investment Treaties and Investor Corruption: An Emerging Defence for Host States?' (2011-2012) 52 *Va. J. Int'l L.* 723-746.

Yannaca-Small C 'Definition of Investor and Investment in International Investment Agreements' 2008 *OECD* 1-100.

Websites

Anderson S 'The New U.S Model Bilateral Investment Treaty: A Public Interest Critique' available at *http://www.ipsdc.org/the_new_us_model_bilateral_investment_treaty_a_public_interest_critique/*(accessed 4 March 2015).

Baruti R 'Building International Investment Law Expertise For Africa' available at *http://www.innovatingjustice.com/innovations/building-international-investment-law-expertise-for-africa* (Accessed 20 March 2015).

Brumfield B 'Garissa University Attack: The Problems Plaguing Kenya's Security Efforts' available at *http://edition.cnn.com/2015/04/03/africa/garissa-attacks-kenya-security/* (accessed 3 April 2015).

Bernasconi-Osterwalder N & Johnson L 'Commentary to the Austrian Model Investment Treaty' available at *http://media.arbeiterkammer.at/wien/PDF/studien/Studie_Investitionsschutzabkommen_en.pdf* (accessed 3 March 2015).

Bland B & Donnan S 'Indonesia to terminate more than 60 bilateral investment treaties' available at *http://www.ft.com/intl/cms/s/0/3755c1b2-b4e2-11e3-af92-00144feabdc0.html#axzz3WrEMIGn5* (accessed 2 March 2015).

Budget Information Programme Team 'The Budget Focus Issue No 30' available at *www.ieakenya.or.ke/publications/doc_download/246-tax-incentives-and-exemption-regime-in-kenya-is-it-working* (accessed 5 March 2015).

Canada's Coalition to end Global Poverty 'Bilateral Investment Treaties: A Canadian Primer' available at *http://www.ccic.ca/_files/en/what_we_do/trade_2010-04_investmt_treaties_primer_e.pdf* (accessed 3 March 2015).

Carrim X 'Lessons from South Africa's Bilateral Investment Treaties Review' available at *http://ccsi.columbia.edu/files/2013/10/No_109_-_Carim_-_FINAL.pdf* (accessed 4 March, 2015).

Carrim X 'South Africa and Bilateral Investment Treaties' available at *www.thetradebeat.com%2Fdoc_download%2F17-south-africa-and-bilateral-investment-treaties* (accessed 4 March 2015).

Columbia Centre on Sustainable Investment 'Local Content South Africa- Mining & Petroleum' available at *http://ccsi.columbia.edu/files/2014/03/Local-Content-South-Africa-Mining-and-Petroleum-CCSI-Feb-2015.pdf* (accessed 5 March 2015).

Cotula L 'Is the tide turning for Africa's investment treaties?' available at http://www.iied.org/tide-turning-for-africa-s-investment-treaties(Accessed 19 October 2014).

Cowley R & Bridi A 'Investor Corruption Bilateral Investment Treaties and International Arbitration: Bribery at Centre of Failed Investor Claim' available at *http://www.nortonrosefulbright.com/knowledge/publications/111529/investor-corruption-bilateral-investment-treaties-and-international-arbitration-bribery-at-centre-of-failed* (accessed 20 March 2015).

De Gama M M 'South Africa's Promotion and Protection of Investment Bill' available at *www.saiia.org.za%2Fdoc_download%2F688-2015-02-16-fdi-presentation-dr-mustaqeem-de-gama* (accessed 3 March 2015).

Draper P 'Africa: South Africa's Termination of Bilateral Investment Treaties Featured' available at *http://allafrica.com/stories/201309301804.html* (accessed on 27 February 2015).

Feris J 'Challenging the Status quo- South Africa`s termination of its Bilateral Trade Agreements' available at *https://www.dlapiper.com/en/latinamerica/insights/publications/2014/12/international-arbitration-newsletter-q4-2014/challenging-the-status-quo/* (accessed 3 March 2015).

Green A R 'Bilateral investment treaties coming back to bite' available at *http://www.thisisafricaonline.com/Business/Legal-Bulletin/Bilateral-investment-treaties-coming-back-to-bite*(Accessed 20 March 2015).

Gundan F 'Kenya Joins Africa's Top 10 Economies After Rebasing of its Gross Domestic Product (GDP)' available at *http://www.forbes.com/sites/faraigundan/2014/10/01/kenya-joins-africas-top-10-economies-after-rebasing-of-its-gross-domestic-product/* (accessed 25 March 2015).

Hovells, Nesbitt, Gonzalez et al 'Indonesia terminates its Bilateral Investment Treaties (BIT) with the Netherlands from the 1st of July 2015 and may terminate all of its BIT's' available at http://www.lexology.com/library/detail.aspx?g=2a596886-3ad2-464b-a510-ab3b0cff503b (Accessed 19/09/2014).

Holman Fenwick Willan 'Kenya- Mining Update' available at *http://www.hfw.com/downloads/HFW-Kenya-Mining-September-2013.pdf* (accessed on 23 February 2015).

Indonesia for Global Justice 'After South Africa, Indonesia takes a brave decision to terminate its BIT with the Netherlands' available at *http://www.bilaterals.org/?press-release-indonesia-takes-a* (accessed 2 March 2015).

Investment Treaty News 'South Africa begins withdrawing from EU-member BITs' available at *http://www.iisd.org/itn/2012/10/30/news-in-brief-9/* (accessed 5 March 2015).

Kariuki J 'Kenya told to review bilateral trade agreements' available at http://www.nation.co.ke/business/Kenya-told-to-review-trade-deals/-/996/2452122/-/hwnj81/-/index.html(Accessed 19 October 2014).

Khisa I 'Talks on EAC-US trade, investment deal face hurdles' available at *http://www.theeastafrican.co.ke/business/-investment-deal-face-hurdles/-/2560/2451498/-/item/0/-/qfferbz/-/index.html* (accessed 4 March 2015).

Kimeni M S & Kibe J 'Africa's Powerhouse' available at *http://www.brookings.edu/research/opinions/2013/12/30-kenya-economy-kimenyi* (accessed 20 March 2015).

King and Spalding Client Alert 'Recent Developments: Kenya- What legal options are available to mining companies' available at *http://www.kslaw.com/imageserver/KSPublic/library/publication/ca082013.pdf*(accessed 20 April 2015).

Kolver L 'South Africa proceeds with termination of bilateral investment treaties' availbale at *http://www.wti.org/fileadmin/user_upload/wti.org/00_Press_Downloads/SA_proceeds_with_termination_of_bilateral_investment_treaties.pdf* (accessed 3 March 2015).

KPMG 'Kenya Country Profile' available at *http://www.kpmg.com/Africa/en/KPMG-in-Africa/Documents/Kenya.pdf* (accessed 20 April 2015).

Lang J 'Bilateral Investment Treaties- a shield or a sword?' available at *http://www.bowman.co.za/FileBrowser/ArticleDocuments/South-African-Government-Canceling-Bilateral-Investment-Treaties.pdf* (accessed 4 March 2015).

Langalanga A 'South Africa's Foreign Investment Regulation: A Revisit' available at *http://blogaila.com/2013/12/05/south-africas-foreign-investment-regulation-a-revisit-by-azwimpheleli-langalanga/* (accessed 24 March 2015).

Lester S 'Improving Investment Treaties through General Exceptions Provisions: The Australian Example' available at *http://www.iisd.org/sites/default/files/publications/iisd_itn_may_2014_en.pdf* (accessed 25 March 2015).

Masamba M 'Africa and Bilateral Investment Treaties: to "BIT"or Not' available at *http://www.consultancyafrica.com/index.php?option=com_content&view=article&id=1697:africa-and-bilateral-investment-treaties-to-bit-or-not&catid=82:african-industry-a-business&Itemid=266*

National TV Kenya 'UNCTAD's Sec. Gen. Dr Mukhisa Kituyi calls for Kenya to review her Bilateral agreements' available at *http://mtaani.com/videochannel/43366/unctads-sec-gen-dr-mukhisa-kituyi-calls-for-kenya-to-review-her-bilateral-a/* (accessed 25 February 2015).

Nelson Mandela Foundation 'Address by Nelson Mandela at HJ Heinz Company Foundation Distinguished Lecture, Pennsylvania- United States' available at *http://www.mandela.gov.za/mandela_speeches/1991/911206_heinz.htm* (Accessed 3 March 2015).

Ong`onge L 'Why Kenya should not sign any more Bilateral Investment Treaties' available at *http://www.ieakenya.or.ke/blog/why-kenya-should-not-sign-any-more-bilateral-investment-treaties* (accessed 20 April 2015).

Parly Report SA 'Promotion and Protection of Investment Bill opens up major row' available at *http://parlyreportsa.co.za/finance-economic/promotion-and-protection-of-investment-bill-opens-major-row/* (Accessed 20 March 2015).

Press Release 'East Africa: First Round of Negotiations by Regional Negotiating Forum on the COMESA Common Investment Area' available at *http://allafrica.com/stories/200503231018.html* (accessed 20 March 2015).

Qureshi K Q C 'Bilateral Investment Treaties (BITs): The Essentials' available at *www.mcnairchambers.com/media/.../InvestmentTreatyEssentials_.pdf (accessed 26 February 2015).*

Reuters 'South Africa Investment Law Overhaul Sparks Concerns' available at *http://www.safpi.org/news/article/2013/south-africa-investment-law-overhaul-sparks-concerns* (Assessed 20 March 2015).

Ruff D, Kron J & Golsong C 'Bilateral Investment Treaties in South Africa' available at *http://www.nortonrosefulbright.com/knowledge/publications/118456/bilateral-investment-treaties-in-south-africa* (accessed 3 March 2015).

Salomon C, Friedrich S & Latham & Watkins International Arbitration Group 'How Most Favoured Nation Clauses in Bilateral Investment Treaties Affect Arbitration' available at *http://www.lw.com/thoughtLeadership/favoured-nation-clauses-arbitration* (accessed 25 March 2015).

South Africa Info 'Black Economic Empowerment' available at *http://www.southafrica.info/business/trends/empowerment/bee.htm#.VP8F78s5DIU#ixzz3Tzozbky6* (accessed 3 March 2015).

South Africa Info 'Bill provides "robust protection" for investors' available at *http://www.southafrica.info/business/investing/regulations/protection-bill-051113.htm#.VTKVQiFViko* (accessed 4 March 2015).

Stafford J 'All Eyes On Kenya: The Next Big Oil Exporter' available at *http://oilprice.com/Energy/Crude-Oil/All-Eyes-on-Kenya-The-Next-Big-Oil-Exporter.html* (accessed 20 March 2015).

Tanzi V & Zee H 'Tax Policy for Developing Countries' available at *http://www.imf.org/external/pubs/ft/issues/issues27/* (accessed 25 February 2015).

Tax Justice Network- Africa and ActionAid International 'Tax Competition in East Africa: A Race to the Bottom? Tax incentives and revenue losses in Kenya' available at *http://www.taxjustice.net/cms/upload/pdf/kenya_report_full.pdf* (accessed 15 March 2015).

Trade Law Centre 'Training Programme-Drafting and Negotiating Investment Treaties: Zimbabwe, August 2014' available at *http://www.tralac.org/events/article/6085-training-programme-drafting-and-negotiating-investment-treaties-zimbabwe-august-2014* (accessed 20 March 2015).

UNCTAD 'Division on Investment and Enterprise' available at http://unctad.org/en/Pages/DIAE/Foreign-Direct-Investment-(FDI).aspx(Accessed on 27 October 2014).

UNCTAD 'Investment Instruments Online' available at http://www.unctadxi.org/templates/Page1006.aspx (Accessed 19 October 2014).

UNCTAD 'Investment policy hub' available at *http://investmentpolicyhub.unctad.org/IIA/CountryBits/108*(accessed 25 February 2015).

UNCTAD 'Recent developments in investor-state disputes ISDS' Issue note number 1 May 2013 available at *http://unctad.org/en/publicationslibrary/webdiaepcb2013d3_en.pdf*(accessed 25 February 2015).

UNCTAD 'Recent developments in investor state disputes ISDS' Issue note number 1 April 2014 available at http://unctad.org/en/publicationslibrary/webdiaepcb2014d3_en.pdf(Accessed 19 October 2014).

UNCTAD 'South Africa Bilateral Investment Treaties' available at *http://investmentpolicyhub.unctad.org/IIA/CountryBits/195#iiaInnerMenu* (accessed 3 March 2015).

UNCTAD 'Speaking notes for workshop on Capital Account Regulations and Global Economic Governance UNCTAD/WTO, Geneva 3-4 October' available at *http://unctad.org/meetings/en/Presentation/UNCTAD-GEGI-Carim-2013.pdf* (accessed 3 March 2015).

U.S Department of State 'Investment Climate Statement 2014' available at *http://www.state.gov/e/eb/rls/othr/ics/2014/index.htm* (accessed 20 April 2015).

Utterback M, Carroll M & Rich E 'Bribery and Corruption in Foreign Investment: Investor beware' available at *http://www.chinalawinsight.com/2014/08/articles/dispute-resolution/bribery-and-corruption-in-foreign-innvestments-investor-beware/* (accessed 20 April 2015).

Vis-Dunbar D 'Advisory Committee Submits report on the United States Model Bilateral Investment Treaty' available at *http://www.iisd.org/itn/2009/10/01/advisory-committee-submits-report-on-the-united-states-model-bilateral-investment-treaty/* (accessed 4 March 2015).

Williams R 'Nothing Sacred: Developing Countries and the future of International Investment Treaties' available at *http://www.iisd.org/pdf/2011/developing_countries_and_the_future_of_IIAs.pdf* (accessed 3 March 2015).

Woolfrey S 'Another BIT bites the dust' available at *http://www.tralac.org/discussions/article/5342-another-bit-bites-the-dust.html* (accessed 20 March 2015).

Woolfrey S 'South Africa's Promotion and Protection of Investment Bill' available at *http://www.tralac.org/discussions/article/5345-south-africa-s-promotion-and-protection-of-investment-bill.html*(accessed 4 March 2015).

Woolfrey S 'South Africa's stance on Bilateral Investment Treaties' available at *http://www.tralac.org/discussions/article/5287-south-africa-s-stance-on-bilateral-investment-treaties.html* (accessed on 3 March 2015).

Theses

Butler N 'The State of International Investment Arbitration: The Possibility of Establishing An Appeal Mechanism' (unpublished Ph.D thesis, The University of Leeds, 2012).

Haftel Y & Thompson A *When Do States Renegotiate International Agreements? The Case of Bilateral Investment Treaties* (working paper, University of Maryland 2013).

Klaaren J & Schneiderman D *Investor-State Arbitration and South Africa's Bilateral Investment Treaty Policy Framework Review* (comment submitted to the DTI, Mandela Institute 2009).

Mossallam M *Process matters: South Africa's experience exiting its BITs* (GEG working paper, University of Oxford 2015/97).

Poulsen L N S *Sacrificing Sovereignty by Chance: Investment Treaties, Developing Countries and Bounded Rationality* (unpublished Ph.D thesis, London School of Economics and Political Science, 2011).

Government Papers

Government Position Paper *Bilateral Investment Treaty Policy Framework Review* (2009) Department of Trade and Industry: Pretoria

Cases

Antoine Goetz and Others v The Republic of Burundi ICSID Case No. ARB/01/2

CMS Gas Transmission Co. v The Republic of Argentina. (ICSID Case No. ARB/01/8)

Fraport AG Frankfurt Airport Services Worldwide *v The Republic of Philippines* ICSID Case No. ARB/03/25

Maffezini v Spain ICSID Case No. ARB/97/7

Metalclad Corporation v The United Mexican States ICSID Case No. ARB(AF)/97/1

Metal-Tech Ltd v Republic of Uzbekistan ICSID Case No. ARB/10/3

Piero *Foresti*, Laura de Carli & Others v. The Republic of *South Africa*, ICSID *Case*No. ARB(AF)/07/01

Saipem S.p.A v The Peoples Republic of Bangladesh ICSID Case No. ARB/05/07

Spentex Netherlands B. V v the Republic of Uzbekistan ICSID Case No. ARB/13/26.

Swiss Investor v. Republic of South Africa, UNCITRAL

Tokios Tokeles v Ukraine ICSID Case No. ARB/02/18

Waguih Elie George Siag and Clorinda Vecchi v The Arab Republic of Egypt ICSID Case No. ARB/05/15.

World Duty-Free Company v The Republic of Kenya ICSID Case No. ARB/00/7

Treaties

Vienna convention on the Laws of Treaties, 1969 (1969) 8 ILM.

Kenya's Bilateral Investment Treaties

Treaty between the Federal Republic of Germany and the Republic of Kenya concerning the Encouragement and Reciprocal Protection of Investments of 1996.

Agreement on Economic Co-operation between the Government of the Kingdom of the Netherlands and the Government of the Republic of Kenya of 1970.

Agreement between the Government of the United Kingdom of Great Britain and Northern Ireland and the Government of the Republic of Kenya for the Promotion and Protection of Investments of 2000.

South Africa's Bilateral Investment Treaties

Agreement on encouragement and reciprocal protection of investments between the Republic of South Africa and the Kingdom of the Netherlands of 1995

Treaty Between the Federal Republic of Germany and the Republic or South Africa concerning the reciprocal Encouragement and Protection of Investment of 1995

Agreement between the government of the Republic of Korea and the government of the Republic of South Africa on the promotion and protection of investment of 1995

Legislation

Kenya's Legislation

Foreign Investment Protection Act 35 of 1964

Export Processing Zone Act Chapter 157 of 1990.

The 'Mining Bill' published in Kenya Gazette Supplement No 28 National Assembly Bills No 8.

South Africa's Legislation

Constitution of the Republic of South Africa 108 of 1996

The *Protection and Promotion of Investment Bill* (GN 1087 in GG 36995 of 1 November 2013).